10-Minute Stories From World Mythology: Egypt, Mesopotamia, and Norse

Glorious and Mystical Heroes like Beowulf, Gilgamesh, Horus, and Thor

Joy Chester

Contents

Perface

Children nowadays seem to read less and less. Reading a book can seem like a chore when entertainment can be gained through a screen so much more easily. But studies have shown that developing an "atomic habit" - just doing ten minutes a day of whatever skill or habit you want to take on can be more than enough to engrain it into our lives. Therefore, we have transformed timeless, legendary stories into 10-minute, bite-size chunks, which are long enough to entertain, enthral, and even educate the reader but are short enough to be enjoyed quickly at bedtime or at any other point in our busy modern days. Within a matter of weeks, reading just 10 minutes a day, children can develop a habit that will benefit their lives immeasurably. It starts with just the turn of a page.

This is the third in our series on Ancient Myths. Our first two books revolved around the cradle of European civilization: Greece. But the Greeks were not the only ones whose songs were sung around the fire, whose tales have echoed down the ages. It is time to stretch our narrative wings and, like Odin's ravens or Zeus' eagle, travel to far-flung lands and hear their stories as well. This, therefore, is the first volume in our series on World Mythology, starting in the lands of Sweden, Norway, and Denmark, Egypt, and modern-day Iraq, Iran, and Syria. The Epic of Gilgamesh was literally set in stone perhaps 3,800 years ago, and Beowulf's saga is the first extant piece of (Old) English written, penned about 1,000 years ago. Meanwhile, our recorded knowledge of Egyptian culture dates back 5,000 years, and we know that the Nile valley was inhabited for at least 2,000 years before that as well. Thus the tales of Ra and Set and Isis are ancient in the extreme. In short, these tales have survived an unimaginably long time for good reason: they are truly wondrous.

From the Fertile Crescent of the Tigris and Euphrates, along the banks of the mighty River Nile, to the deep, narrow fjords of Sweden and Denmark, heroes, monsters, and gods have trekked and battled and, above all, searching for deeper meaning in their own lives. The peoples of Mesopotamia, Scandinavia, and Egypt saw and imagined the world very differently. Each part begins with a creation myth to evoke the individual cultural identities of each geographical area, hopefully inspiring images and feelings just as clear and distinct as those of chariots, longships, and reed boats. Beowulf and Gilgamesh, Osiris and Thor are names that have reverberated through time just as vividly as those of Herakles and Odysseus, but while these characters are all gloriously heroic, they are also very much their own people. Each character is superbly different in strengths, weaknesses, goals, and locations, but they are all equally human.

Each chapter can stand alone or be read in order. You could enjoy them at bedtime, in the car, on a plane, wherever you like. That's the magic of these tales; you can take them with you anywhere! Some of the more gruesome or difficult details have been left aside, lying ready in the original texts for the adventurous soul who wants to dive in, having been hooked by the gripping tales in this book. That's the hope, anyway, for these are some of the greatest stories ever told. There is a whole world out there, ready to be discovered.

So, as we have said before, dear reader, be ready to be thrilled, excited, scared, disgusted, confused, enthralled, and delighted. We truly envy you because you are about to read these stories for the very first time, and that is a special moment. Take a deep breath and dive on in.

Part I: Egypt

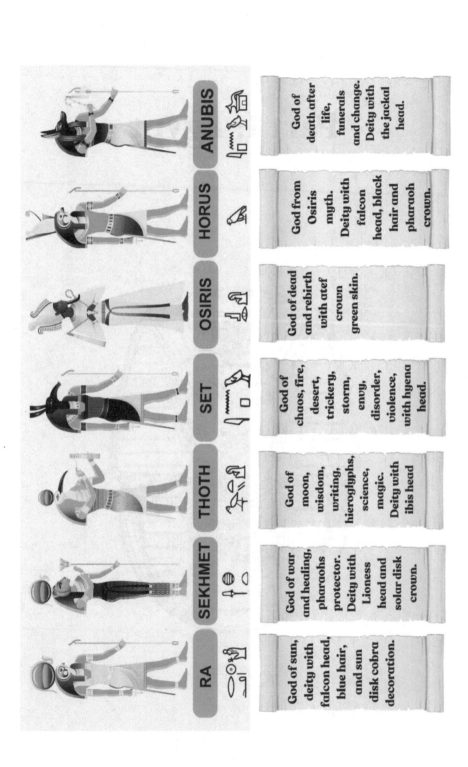

Chapter 1: From Horizon to Horizon.

"There is only water, and I am that water." said Nun, and for eons of time this was true. Nun knew nothing more than this, for there was no light, no dark, just Nun. But then, out of the void of water that was Nun, there came a second voice, and Nun knew that things would never be the same again. "I am land, and I am Geb." Geb was flat and vast, not as vast as the infinite Nun, but great, as dry and rugged as Nun was smooth and wet. "I am Nun, and you are Geb." said Nun.

"There is only us." rumbled Geb in agreement.

But then a third, higher voice came, and Nun and Geb knew that things would never be the same again. "I am the sky which arches above, and I am Nut." cried the third voice. Over Nun the water and Geb the land lay Nut the sky, until a fourth voice came, and Nun and Geb and Nut knew that things would never be the same again.

"I am the air, and I am Shu." breathed the voice, and the first wind rippled the surface of the water, caught up the sand from the land,

and raised Nut high, high above them all. Shu the air stood on Geb the land and held Nut the sky high above them, even above Nun the water. But still, there was no light, no dark, just Nun and Geb and Nut and Shu.

The four of them existed. They had no way of telling how long they were there, and it did not matter to them. But then light came. Far to one side of Nun the sea it came, rising high above Geb the land and passing through Nut the sky and Shu the air. The four beings were powerless to stop the light, which was focused in a great disc, so bright that they could scarcely see its true color. "I am Ra. I am the sun. I bring light to the world." And Nun and Geb and Nut and Shu knew that things would never be the same again. Staring at the bright disc, they saw that it was carried on the head of a great creature, with the body of a man but the head of a mighty falcon. This was Ra, the god of the sun. He did not walk nor fly but sat aboard a huge reed barge.

"What is the world?" they asked as one.

"You are. We are. And so will they be." replied Ra.

"Who are they?" asked the four.

Ra smiled an unknowable smile. "Whoever I decide. But that must wait until tomorrow."

Glancing at each other, confused and concerned, Nun and Geb asked, "What is tomorrow?"

The falcon-headed god pointed first behind his barge, beyond the edge of Nun, and then traced a semi-circular course straight ahead to the other side of Nun. "I rose in the east and will set in the west.

When that is done, I shall step off this Mandjet, this solar barge of the day, and step onto the Mesektet, the solar barge of the night. I shall then sail through the Duat until I return to the Mandjet and sail from east to west again. When I do this, it shall be tomorrow or rather today."

Nut and Shu were as confused as the other two. "But there is nothing other than us: than Nun and Geb, Nut and Shu."

Ra shook his head, neither angrily nor calmly, neither happily nor sadly. "There is the Duat. You shall never see it, for you must remain here forever. But just as you are here, the Duat is there."

As they spoke, the Mandjet, the solar barge of the day, continued to bear Ra slowly through the sky inexorably towards the west. As he neared the edge of Nun, he turned back and shouted, "See you tomorrow. Enjoy the night!"

But before any of them could ask him what "night" was, Ra and the Mandjet disappeared beyond the edge of Nun, and night enveloped them in darkness so complete that they forgot what light was.

"When will he return?" Cried Nun, his voice echoing into the never-ending blackness. Neither Geb nor Nut nor Shu had the answer but all quailed in fear as the night stretched onwards. Finally, a single tiny gemstone of light flashed at the far end of Nun, and the Mandjet, the great solar barge of the day edged over the horizon again, bringing Ra and the glorious brightness of the sun again. Ra smiled down at them. "Good morning! There is much to do today." And thus, he began a great labor. The four beings did not care, so happy were they to have the light back. Ra was, in the meantime, busy.

He planted trees upon Geb the land, built hills, and dug valleys. Parts of Geb he left dry and sandy; parts were as lush and full of life as can be imagined. He spread white, fluffy clouds across Nut the sky, and let some of them drop water in thousands of tiny droplets wherever they wished. He taught Geb and Shu how to create birds, plants, and animals of such variety that the four beings could only gape. But he had not forgotten Nun: He let islands, great and small, rise up out of the depths of the water, and just as Geb and Shu could bring forth life on land and in the air, so Nun learned to create fish to swim and underwater plants to fill the deeps of the sea just as the trees grew and animals ran across the land.

In the very middle of the world, Ra dug a great river, so long and beautiful that the other beings cried out in wonder. The soil through which it ran was dark and rich, and no sooner had Ra laid it and filled it with fresh water than all manner of living things flocked to it. Settling back on his solar barge, Ra nodded contentedly. "This is the Nile." he told them. "It is no god, but it is the jewel that shall keep the world alive. Tomorrow will be a great new day, but now I must go to the Duat."

Ra was just waving farewell when Nun and Geb, Nut, and Shu realized what was to come and cried aloud in fear. "Do not leave us in the dark, great Ra of the Two Horizons! The night is terrible and dark." The Mandjet was just reaching the edge of Nun when Ra turned back, a thoughtful look on his face. With one finger, he flicked a tiny jewel of light up to Nut, saying, "Make more of these, Nut. These are your children and will light the world while I am away." With that he was gone, and the darkness plunged around them again, save for that tiny pinprick of light in Nut's hand. As the night wore on, Nut made more and more of the star-jewels and spread them across herself, gently lighting the world around them.

As the days and nights went by, Ra continued to fill the world with living creatures, particularly humans, who rejoiced at the wonderful richness of the "Black Land", the fertile soils surrounding the river Nile, and marveled at the strange beauty of the "Red Land", the wide deserts that lay beyond. But Nun and Geb and Nut and Shu were not idle any more, either, and soon new gods came from their unions. There came Isis, goddess of magic and cunning, who looked like a beautiful woman with feathers coming from her arms like a cloak; Tall Osiris, god of fertility and farming, whose handsomeness was striking; Set, a hyena-headed god of deserts and storms. Many others followed, and the four original beings were not the only ones to make more children. Soon came Sekhmet, a fire-breathing goddess with the head of a lioness, Anubis the jackal-headed with skin as dark as night, and Thoth, the ibis-headed god of the moon, wisdom, and magic.

Ra sat in royal court above them all, the sun shining its life-giving warmth down upon them all, from his solar barge. The day wore on, and he called upon Set to join him as he headed westwards. As the Mandjet sank beneath the western horizon, Nun turned to the ibis-headed Thoth. "What is the Duat? Why does Ra go down there every night?"

*Thoth, the ibis-headed god of
the moon, wisdom, and magic.*

The smile faded from Thoth's face to be replaced by a shadow of fear and concern. "You don't want to know."

Chapter 2: The Truth of Ra

Ra, the god of the sun

D ays passed, then months, then years. The gods lived in happiness, watching the mortal beings grow, multiply, age, and die. This was the way of things. Those who died entered the Duat, the Underworld, but few of the immortals lived or journeyed there and returned. Anubis, the dark-skinned, jackal-headed god, was one of these. His role was to help those who had died to pass into the Duat, where they would face judgment based on how they had lived their lives. Ra, the falcon-headed sun god, and Set, the hyena-headed god of storms and deserts, were two who, as night beckoned, would ride the Mandjet, Ra's solar barge, into the west. Once beyond the horizon, they would ride the Mesektet, the solar barge of the night, through the Duat. What else was their purpose there few knew, and n one would speak of it.

Another goddess who sometimes joined Ra and Set on the Mandjet westwards was Sekhmet, Ra's daughter. A formidable figure with the head of a lioness, Sekhmet's temper was as fiery as her breath, which could cause plagues and disease as well as forest fires. Few of the gods would dare prompt her rage, although an unlikely friendship existed between her and Shu, the air.

As time passed, many of the gods began to notice that Ra, who ruled the world by day as well as sailing the Duat by night, was starting to age. His hair, once a deep blue, began to become streaked with white. There were times when he seemed so tired that he would rest under his favorite tree: the lavender-like jacaranda tree. But the sun still shined just as brightly, and the Nile flooded every year as it always did, bringing fresh, dark soil to the Black Land along its banks where crops grew tall and plentiful. So, no-one worried too much.

There came a day, however, when something strange, even frightening, happened, and the gods knew that things would never be the same again. As the gods sat in council on a wide porch at the front of the great palace of Ra, a friendly debate was being held between Thoth, the ibis-headed god of the moon, and Nut, the sky, over which stars should go into which constellations. The other gods were laughing as Thoth jokingly suggested one ridiculous suggestion after another. "No!" he said, "You're looking at it upside down. That is clearly a hippo, never an eagle!"

A loud snore punctuated Nut's response, and all turned to see that Ra, whose hair now contained more grey and white hairs than blue, had fallen asleep in his throne. Not knowing quite what to say, many of the gods laughed anew, so strange and amusing was the sight of the mighty, falcon-headed sun god dozing in his throne. Sekhmet alone, however, did not smile. As Thoth nudged Anhur, the god of war, and whispered something, Sekhmet leaped to her feet and hurled her goblet at Ra's feet. Waking with a start, Ra stared around with bleary e yes.

"How dare you sleep at council?!" She roared. "How dare you disrespect your office so?" Ra straightened in his seat, rubbing his eyes, and would have responded had she not carried on, spraying spit from her bared fangs. "I have had enough of your laziness. You are the sun! You cannot close your eyes for an instant, for you bring life to this world. I will go now and find another more worthy of the sun-disk!" With that, she stalked out, her amber eyes flashing.

At that moment, the sun itself seemed to dim, if only slightly, and Ra slumped in his throne as though at a loss for words. Set, his temper nearly as potent as Sekhmet's, sprang to Ra's side. "She must

be brought back at once, my lord!" Ra frowned, and Thoth stood as w
ell.

"Let her cool off, and then she shall return. We all know what it is
like to lose our temper."

The crease in Ra's forehead deepened.

"We need her back, Lord of the Two Horizons!" insisted the hyena-headed deity. "You know we do."

Some of the gods gasped as Ra, too, got to his feet, for he was
suddenly unsteady, if only for a moment. "You are both right." he
said, and his voice was as strong as it was before. "Let her come back
of her own accord. It will be better so."

Set shook his head but did not dare argue with the sun god. That
evening, he and Ra boarded the Mandjet and headed into the west.

But Sekhmet did not return the next day, nor the day after that. Ra
spent much time on the solar barge, alternating between searching
the many lands which flowed beneath him like stones and reeds in a
riverbed, and sleeping. Yes, Ra slept, and each day another white hair
bloomed across his head. While he rested his eyes, the sun seemed to
dim, as though a cloud had passed over it. The gods worried as they
had never before, and on the third day, as they sat in council, Isis, the
feather-armed wife of Osiris, dared to ask what none had dared to as
k before.

"Lod of the Two Horizons, what ails you? Where has Sekhmet
gone? What is it that you do in the Duat all night? Is that what tires
you so?"

Ra's eyes flashed. "You forget your place, Isis. Nothing ails me. But it is time for Sekhmet to return to my palace." He turned to Thoth and Anhur. "You two shall head east. At the head of the Sea of Calm you shall find my daughter."

The two of them glanced at each other, sharing a combination of anxiety, confusion, and surprise. "My king," said Anhur, tentatively, "what if she will not come willingly?"

"I have told you to bring her back." snapped Ra. "Alive. How you do this is up to you. Now go!" His fist slammed onto the armrest of his throne and all present felt that blow. The two gods, of the moon and of war, turned and left. Mounting their chariots, they would have whipped up the horses to leap away, had Set not called them to wait.

"Lord of the Red Land!" called Anhur. "Are you coming with us?"

The hyena-headed god shook his head. "I cannot. Ra needs me in the Duat. That is why I come, to beg you to hurry on your mission. Do not stop even to rest."

Anhur's temper flared. "By the Nile, tell us! What is wrong with Ra? Why do you sail the Mandjet into the west? What is it that you do in the Duat every night?"

Set glanced nervously over his shoulder and then back to them. "Sekhmet is more than Ra's daughter. She is his Eye." he whispered.

Only Thoth didn't look confused at this strange statement.

"But he has two..." began Anhur.

"She is the Eye of Ra – she is part of his power. Why do you think the sun keeps shining when Ra sleeps? Desert and river, leaf and root, hunter and prey, woman and man, there are pairs throughout the world. Sekhmet is as much the sun as Ra is, and without her he is weakened. She must be brought home soon, or all is lost."

"You seem to understand this all," grumbled Thoth, "so why aren't you going after her?"

Sparks flashed in Set's palms as he turned to the ibis-headed god of magic, "Have you never noticed the earthquakes that rock the mountains by day and night? Where do they come from; do you think? There is far more to the world than you can ever realize, you with your head in the clouds. Beneath us, in the Duat, there are more than just those who have died and passed on. Beneath us lies Apophis." At the mention of that name, each deity shivered, though they had never heard it before. "He is the lord of Chaos, the great serpent, the gulf that swallows light, the eater of souls. He is the enemy of Ra and of us all. Every night Ra goes into the Duat and does battle with Apophis, keeping the beast at bay for another day. Sekhmet and I often join him, for Apophis is great and, unlike Ra, he does not have to keep the world alive as well. Without Sekhmet, Ra is weaker, and the battles take a heavier toll on him. That is why I cannot go. That is why you must be swift!"

Thoth and Anhur stood for a moment, stunned at the hammering truth which Set had delivered. This was why Ra was aging so quickly, and why the sun had dimmed as Sekhmet had left. Taking up his reins, Anhur rolled his shoulders and fixed his eyes on the wide lands before them. "And I think we have another problem." he muttered.

"What now?" cried Thoth. "Isn't it bad enough that we have to drag Sekhmet back here?"

"It could be worse." The war-god shook his head, almost sadly. "There is unrest in the land. The humans are afraid, and when humans are afraid, they fight."

"Why should that worry you? You literally live for war!" laughed Set.

"Because" replied Anhur, scowling, "they won't be fighting with each other. I sense more than war. I sense rebellion. We must hurry, or all of humanity will be at our gates."

Crying aloud to their horses, the two gods cracked their whips and, with stones spitting from their wheels, they flew, as though on wings, into the north. High above, Set and Ra sat aboard the Mandjet. Ra lay with eyes closed, a frown of concern creasing his face, while Set plied the tiller, steering them across the waves of wind and cloud towards the western horizon. As though with a sense no mortal could wield, Set could feel the ground beneath them quiver as the coils of Apophis shifted in the Duat. The hyena-headed god gripped the thick wood of the steering bar and shook away his fear. Far below he could see the two chariots skipping over the wide plains. "Go, my brothers." he whispered. "I don't know how many more nights we can keep the great serpent at bay!"

Chapter 3: The Wrath of Sekhmet

Sekhmet, a fire-breathing goddess
with the head of a lioness

S ent to bring Sekhmet, the Eye of Ra, back to the palace, Anhur
and Thoth sped eastwards in their swift chariots. Ra's palace

stood just south of the beginning of the Great Delta, where the Nile spread its waters wide across the flats as it met the sea. That place was called Shesepibre, or "Joy of Ra", and from there they drove, first speeding through the lush farmlands of the Black Land where the Nile flooded each year to bring fresh, dark soil and live-giving water to the farms of Egypt. But their hearts were uneasy, not only due to their dangerous errand – Sekhmet was a powerful goddess whose wrath was legendary – but also because of the unfriendly eyes turned in their direction.

The men and women whose farms and villages and towns clustered on the banks of the Nile had long lived under the rule of Ra and had been happy. But now a creature stalked the Black Land, invisible but felt by all, silent but heard in every ear. This creature's name was Fear. Everyone had seen the sun's light dim at times, even at midday, and felt the tremors shake the earth as Apophis, Lord of Chaos, the mighty serpent of the Duat, shifted his immeasurable coils. Many among the humans cried that Ra had forsaken them or that the gods were plotting to stop the Nile's annual flood and doom them all to starvation. Neither Thoth nor Anhur had time to stop and reason with the crowds of people, even when they passed a temple which, by accident or design, flamed and fumed, sending a pillar of darkness rising to tarnish the clouds.

"If we cannot rejoin Ra with Sekhmet," shouted Thoth to his companion, "Apophis will be the least of our worries. Even all the gods together cannot face all the peoples of the world!" Anhur did not reply, but neither did he disagree with the moon-god's wisdom.

The wondrous darkness of the Black Land's rich soils was giving way to the sandy expanses of the Red Land, and league after league, their chariots sped ever onward.

Finally, they came to the northernmost point of the Sea of Calm, a long, narrow stretch of water leading to the great Sea of Blood, which marked Egypt's eastern border. To their surprise, Sekhmet was not hard to find. Far ahead they could see the distinctive red linen of her kalasiris among the sparse reeds on the seashore. "Wait a moment." whispered Thoth as they got down from their chariots. Holding a hand aloft, Thoth half-closed his eyes and murmured something the war god could not hear. A gentle breeze from the south wafted over them, cooling the sweat on their shoulders and necks. "Now." Thoth nodded. "That may help calm her."

Anhur nodded his thanks, and together they stepped carefully forwards. The ibis-headed god of magic carried his Was, a long staff with a curiously formed head, like that of a tiny antelope. Anhur alone wore armor and wielded a kopesh, a broad-bladed, sickle-like sword.

Sekhmet lounged on a wide, flat rock at the water's edge, staring out to sea. She did not bother to turn her head as the others approached. "Running messages for Ra now?" she sneered. "Can he no longer summon the energy to get out of his chair, the old fool?"

The war god had drawn his kopesh. Thoth rested a cautioning hand on Anhur's arm. "Sekhmet, come home. You belong with your family."

Stretching like a cat, the lioness-headed goddess turned to face them. "I will decide when I return, not before."

"My friend," hushed Thoth, "You know that Ra needs you to help fight against Apophis. You risk the very destruction of our world! And there is more: the humans are growing rebellious. Temples are already burning. We must stand together as a family!"

Sekhmet growled, "You have spent too much time with Set, my friend. Your tongue has become slippery and sly."

Anhur pulled away from Thoth and stepped forward, hefting his shining kopesh. "Sekhmet, this is madness. Expecting more of your father, that I can understand, but this is just your pride talking now. Get on my chariot now, or I will drag you behind it."

The war god's first error was speaking so aggressively, and his second was trying to grab Sekhmet. Pouncing like a great cat, she hurled him bodily into the water. Thoth stepped backward, frantically brandishing his Was and murmuring a spell of binding. But Sekhmet was bearing down on him, her amber eyes flashing, smoke curling from her nostrils. Opening her jaws, she unleashed a torrent of flame which would have engulfed the moon-god had he not dived to the side. Whirling his Was with a whipping noise, Thoth drew a strange sign in the air as though tracing in the sand. The symbol glowed a fierce red, and then flew at Sekhmet, who countered with more fire from her dripping jaws. The flames could come no closer, but the sweat was pouring down Thoth's long beak as the air around him heated up. With a snap of her teeth, Sekhmet relented, but hurled a rock at Thoth, knocking him to the ground. Scrambling to his knees, he thrust his Was at her again, but Sekhmet leaped away, and before either of them could do anything, she had mounted Anhur's chariot and whipped up the team of horses. "I'm not going back." she snarled as Thoth ran forward. "But I will teach those puny humans a lesson."

Despite his speedily dragging Anhur from the Sea of Calm, Thoth knew they would never catch Sekhmet. The two of them now had to share a single chariot, so they would be slower, and she had a head start. As their tired horses pulled them westwards, the moon-god gasped in despair as they saw more plumes of smoke rising into the air before them. "She is attacking the humans with fire and slaughter!" he cried.

"That is not her way." Anhur disagreed. "She will go among them as a lioness in the night, breathing disease as she goes. But that will be only the beginning of her wrath."

Thoth bowed his head sadly, for Anhur was right. Sekhmet sowed a plague amongst the tribes and towns, never striking in the same area twice. And with her deadly breath she brought more than mere disease, for as death stalked the land, so did fear, doubt and, following on their heels like hyenas smelling a carcass from far off, distrust and greed came ravening into the hearts of man. With so many dead or dying, so few were left to tend the crops and herds. Sekhmet's second weapon was famine, and so the humans who were not ill fought each other over what little food was left. The Black Land was slowly turning red with blood, and Sekhmet, filled with savage triumph, gorged herself on the blood of the slain, coming at night as silent as a shadow so that none knew where she was.

High above in the Mandjet, Ra watched with sleepy eyes as the humans tried to either escape the menace of the plague, store what little food they could find, or fight amongst themselves. The mighty falcon-headed god was full of doubt, for part of him reveled in humanity's suffering: a just punishment for daring to rebel against him. Another part pitied them, for many had died needlessly, and now long stretches of the Nile stood untilled, the empty silence no longer echoing with the sweet laughter of children or the gentle clink of trowel and hoe. A third part of him shook with a fear he had only rarely known in battle with dread Apophis: could he stop Sekhmet, weakened as he was?

It was pity that finally stirred him to action, and his cunning mind offered a path to victory: Taking a huge jar of strong beer, he mixed in a red dye and sent Anhur and Thoth down under cover of darkness to a battlefield to which Sekhmet had not yet come to feast on the blood of the slain. Splashing the blood-red beer in puddles by the fallen, the two gods hid themselves and waited. As the moon rose high above them, they saw the lioness-headed goddess slinking silently among the bodies, a broad smile playing across her face. Triumphant, she drank deeply from the puddle. It was not long before sleep crept over her, and she curled up in a patch of moonlight. With sighs of relief, Anhur and Thoth lifted the sleeping goddess and bore her back to the palace of Ra.

With the sun riding high in the sky, Ra woke his daughter and calmed her rage with soft words. "I am sorry, my child, for the deception played on you, but not for ending your wrathful reign. Humanity has suffered enough. But you were also right: I have tired myself out, battling by night and ruling by day. Even I cannot keep going forever. It is time to take a step back."

Turning to the other assembled gods, he proclaimed. "I shall relinquish direct rule of the mortal world. By day, I shall rest as needed in the Mandjet so that I may continue to keep Apophis at bay. But now I must choose another to take my crown." He paused, and his eyes fell on Set, then Osiris, then Thoth, then Sekhmet, then Anhur, and so on through the company. "Osiris, you shall rule, step forth, and take the throne."

With a growl of rage, Set stepped forward. "Lord of the Two Horizons, I must protest. Have I not served you faithfully all these years and aided you in the battle against the Eater of Souls? Why must I go without reward?"

"Is it not reward enough to fight at my side, Set?" Asked Ra with a stern look at the hyena-headed god. "You already rule the Red Land, but Osiris rules the Black Land. That is where the majority of the humans live, so it makes sense for him to take my crown and govern them in my stead. Besides, I still need you in the Duat. Apophis is a mighty beast, and there are few I would rather have at my side than you."

Set, a hyena-headed god of deserts and storms.

Set bowed his head respectfully and watched as Osiris had the Pschent, the white and red crown of Egypt, bestowed upon him by Ra. But in the heart of the Lord of the Red Land, there came a darkness and a hatred and a rage. "I shall be pharaoh." he promised himself silently. "And all shall bow before me!"

Chapter 4: The Fall of Osiris.

It was now many years since Osiris had taken over the rule of the mortal world from Ra, the sun god. He ruled from Abydos, further south down the Nile than Ra's temple, for he judged it wise. From Abydos, Osiris could reach all corners of Egypt swiftly and rule fairly. While Osiris governed and handed down justice, Ra sailed from the eastern horizon to the west on solar barge, the Mandjet, resting his mind and limbs. For each night he, accompanied often by Set, the god of storms and deserts, or the Eye of Ra, Sekhmet, sailed into the Duat and fought to keep the soul-eating serpent Apophis at bay for one more cycle of sun and moon. He had been aging rapidly from the strain of so much duty, but now he was able to rest and was all the better for it. The rebellious spirit that had flared in the hearts of man had long since subsided, and a sense of contentment and peace filled the kingdom.

But there was one heart that was neither content nor pleased with Osiris' rule: The hyena-headed Set was furious that Ra had not chosen him to be pharaoh in his stead. "I am the one who fights at his side against Apophis!" Raged Set in angry silence. "I am the greatest warrior. I should be pharaoh. I shall be pharaoh!" And so began his plotting and scheming. Set was wise and cunning as well as powerful, and his sharp mind soon found a solution. "I must be careful." he told himself as he sketched out his plan in the bitterness of his thoughts. "Ra rides the Mandjet all day, and while he rests there, he also watches the world beneath him, for he loves it. But he is not all-seeing nor all-knowing. Still, I cannot be even suspected to have had a hand in Osiris' downfall, or all will have been for nothing."

Thus it was, that one day Osiris went hunting in a wide valley, following a herd of gazelle – small, deer-like creatures with long legs and swift ears. With him went many nobles of the towns and tribes around Abydos, and he sent them far up the valley to close around the herd as a net around a shoal of fish. But Osiris and his men were not the only ones hunting that day. A pride of lions slunk silently into the valley. The gazelle, sensing the hungry beasts, fled in panic, leaping and sprinting in all directions so that the hunters often had to jump into trees to avoid being trampled.

Osiris stared through the undergrowth at the bounding, screaming prey and turned to run as several of them, thinking he was the threat, charged with lowered horns as sharp as swords. He was nearly in sight of his chariot when a deep-throated roar split the air like thunder. Heart hammering against his chest, the pharaoh managed to dive out of the way, and the frightened creatures, sensing that terrifying scent on the breeze, careered on. The horses of his chariot maddened with terror, broke free of their reins and galloped off, leaving Osiris coughing in the dust.

The herd was gone, the trees silent. Osiris stood and stared around, not daring to call out for fear of the lions. A soft noise of giant paws made him turn to see a great lioness advancing on him slowly. He backed away but heard a growl reverberating in the air behind him. Everywhere he looked, dark eyes flashed, and long teeth shone in wide, bloody jaws. Something made him pause for a moment: Lions' eyes were normally amber or brown, but these were black. "You have been sent, haven't you?" he asked them quietly, not expecting a response. Then he raised his spear and lunged for the nearest beast with a shout of fury.

The other hunters heard their pharaoh's cry and hurried to the spot, but the roars of wounded lions echoed through the valley, and though they ran with as much speed as their trembling hearts would allow, they came too late. Blood splatted the ground, but there was no sign of the lions. One man, braver than the rest, stepped forwards, looking for any sign of their ruler's body. What he saw made him drop to his knees in horror. The red and white Pschent that normally adorned the pharaoh's brows lay blooded and ripped beside his hunting tunic, which had been slashed and torn. But it was not this that made the hunters weep: the only remains of Osiris, pharaoh of all Egypt, was a single arm. The lions had not eaten him. They had torn his body apart. "They went this way!" shouted one, pointing at a set of tracks.

"No, this way!" cried another, having found more pawprints in the dusty soil.

But their leader shook his head. "The pride has split up, carrying their spoils in all different directions. We shall never find the pharaoh's body now." He knelt and bowed to the one remaining arm up in Osiris' bloody tunic, then reverently picked up the tattered remains of the Pschent.

"We must bear this news back to Abydos!" he said, turning to his friends. "Half of you must remain here and guard our lord's remains. None may touch the, um, the body except for priests of Anubis!" He glanced down at the single limb that was all that remained of the pharaoh and a tear rolled down his cheek. "I shall inform her highness, Isis, and arrange for his majesty to be collected. Be wary, should one of those foul beasts return!" With that, he led a handful of the mourning hunters back the way they had come, leaving the rest on guard, their eyes fearful but watchful.

News of Osiris' death had rocked Abydos and the lands around. Osiris had been well respected by his subjects, who remembered his even-handed sense of justice and his clear sense of organization. Under his rule, the farmlands had grown rich and well-ordered once more, following the great rebellion against Ra. He had not visited terrible punishments on the people but had worked to restore their livelihoods. Now he was gone, and there was little left of him for anyone to mourn. The priests of Anubis, the jackal-headed god of funerals and change, had retrieved the lone arm and brought it back to the palace, where his wife Isis wept long, covering her face with mud, leaving her hair matted and uncared for.

Thoth came to her, his head bowed respectfully. "Isis, it is time to go to the council. The gods must elect a new pharaoh to continue Osiris' good work."

Isis shook her head but said nothing, so Thoth knelt beside her and took her hand.

"Osiris had no heir, did he? So, we must do this. We must move on, Isis, no matter how painful it will be to let go. Let us bury him properly."

"Properly?!" spat Isis, turning furiously to face the ibis-headed god. "How can we bury him properly? We cannot turn him to the west, cannot ensure his mouth is open, so that he may speak to defend himself in the Duat. Without the rest of his body, there can be no rest for my husband. No long, slow sleep of death embalmed."

Thoth eyed her warily. "What are you saying?"

"I shall find him. I shall find every last piece and bring them back to Abydos. Then, and only then, shall I bury him."

Raising his hands to the sky, Thoth said, "You ask the impossible, Isis. The lions who killed him have scattered far and wide. There will be no finding them now."

Rising, Isis strode to the door. "You underestimate me, Thoth."

Isis, goddess of magic and cunning, who looked like a beautiful woman with feathers coming from her arms like a cloak

As she reached the exit, she turned and said, "Doesn't it seem odd to you that a pride of lions would separate after a kill?" Without waiting for an answer, she left, leaving Thoth to walk slowly back to the throne-room, where Ra awaited the last of the gods to arrive. At the window stood Set, trying not to smile as he watched Isis in the courtyard below, summoning horses for her chariot. He knew where she was going and knew that she would fail. His pride of lions had run to the ends of the earth. Some had even dived into seas or climbed high mountains before collapsing with exhaustion. They could not eat the flesh of a god, but they had carried the pieces of Osiris' body so far and wide that they would never be found. Forcing his face into a respectful, neutral expression, he turned back to where the other gods sat assembled.

Ra stood beside the throne, a new Pschent ready in his hands. "My children," he said, "Grief has come unto our family, far more swiftly than even I had guessed. Let Osiris' sad fate stand as a reminder to us all that, although we are immortal, we are still vulnerable to the ways of the world."

He glanced down at the red and white crown in his hands, and tears rolled down his beak to splash on the floor. "Who among you would take on this burden?" he asked. "Dear Isis is not here, so I do not mind saying that it is a pity that Osiris had no heir, though no blame to her can be charged."

He looked around at the circle of gods.

Then Set stood, his hands clasped humbly before him. "Lord of the Two Horizons, once before I asked for the honor, but you said that Osiris was better suited and that you still needed me. I respectfully submit that, now that you have the weight of rule lifted from your shoulders, your days of rest leave you more than ready to battle the dread Serpent of the Duat. Sekhmet aids you as well. But please don't think that I am wary of the battle beneath, rather that I feel myself ready to take on more responsibility. Osiris will be a hard act to follow, but I ask to be allowed the chance to try. It is time for the Black Land and the Red to come under one ruler."

Something in his voice made Thoth wonder, and the parting words of Isis came back to his mind. But already, many of the gods were applauding and nodding their heads, and so Ra gestured that Set should sit in the throne. The Pschent was placed between Set's point-ed ears, and all cried with joy for their new pharaoh. Thoth clapped and smiled with all the rest, but still doubt gnawed at him.

Chapter 5: The Search for Osiris.

Osiris, the first pharaoh of Egypt, was dead, torn apart by a pack of lions. Ra, the falcon-headed sun god, had chosen Set, god of deserts and storms, to rule in his stead. So while Sekhmet took Set's place on the Mandjet, sailing into the Duat each night to aid Ra in his battles with the terrible serpent of the underworld, Apophis, Set ruled. But where Osiris had been just and kind, Set was cruel, commanding the humans not only to farm their land, but also to build a great, triangular building.

"This pyramid," proclaimed Set, "shall stand as a reminder of Osiris: a worthy symbol of his greatness and of the power of the gods."

Thus, it was that under the baking heat of the Egyptian sun, men, women, and children toiled to drag great chunks of stone from the newly dug quarries. These stones were shaped into mighty cubes, each the size of a man, and slowly the pyramid grew taller and taller, as though Set would have it reach the sky. Many collapsed with exhaustion, only to be beaten by the royal guards and forced to their feet again.

The other gods praised Set's devotion to his predecessor, but some worried for the humans lest they rebel against them as they had once tried to overthrow the rule of Ra. When Anhur, the god of war, raised his concerns, Set cackled with mirth, his long tongue lolling out of his mouth. "But that's the beauty of my plan, Anhur: What with the mining of stone, the making of bricks, the building work, on top of farming the land, the humans will be too tired to even try to plot against us. It's a win-win scenario!"

Not everyone rejoiced at Set's work and words, however. Thoth, the ibis-headed god of magic and the moon, made sure to hide his misgivings and his suspicions deep in his heart. But Isis, wife of Osiris, was convinced that there was more to the death of her husband than a simple hunting accident. The pack of lions that had attacked the former pharaoh had done what no pride would ever do: separated and ran away, carrying pieces of their kill with them. Isis was no great hunter, but she had a cunning mind and hands skilled in magic, and so she tracked the beasts across the length and breadth of the world.

Finally, she discovered one of the lions. It had clearly run as far and as fast as it could until its great heart collapsed within its chest, and it fell dead upon the stones. Still in its jaws lay a leg that Isis recognized at once as Osiris'. "Unless they are terrible beasts of the Duat," she told herself, "they cannot possibly eat the flesh of a god. Therefore, Osiris' body is still out there! I will find the other pieces, bring them together, and lay him to rest."

Days became weeks, weeks became months, and still Isis searched. Through dry, sandy deserts and dripping rainforests, through swamps that stank badly enough to make her eyes water, to the tops of mountains and across rocky coastlines. Though her arms ached from weaving spells of finding and her feet were sore from the endless miles, no hardship could quench the fire that burned within her. Each time she found a piece of Osiris, she saw as well that the lion that had borne it so far lay dead but had not rotted away. No vulture, hyena, or other scavenger had dared touch these beasts. Even the worms and insects had left the carcasses alone.

"Some dark magic was at work in you." she told the dead creature one she had extracted Osiris' other arm from its mouth. "I can still sense it. What terrible power drove you to flee from your pride, only to die here, alone and frightened?" She stared around the bare, cold mountainside where she had found the lion and felt a pang of sorrow for the creature's fate, even though it had killed her husband.

The stars were glittering through the window of Thoth's bedroom, and he had just drifted off to sleep when he was shaken awake, a firm hand clamping his long, thin beak shut. Eyes bulging, he thrashed around in his bed and would have drawn a sign of warding if he had not recognized the intruder. Isis, her feathered arms brushing against the sheets, held a slender finger to her lips and then released his beak. Trying to gasp for air quietly, Thoth whispered, "What in the name of the two horizons are you doing, Isis?"

Her eyes were shining in the starlight, her lips trembling with excitement. "I found him, Thoth. I found all the pieces of Osiris!"

Stunned, Thoth took a moment to take this incredible achievement in. No-one, not even Ra, had thought it possible to find Osiris' body again, but Isis had done it. "So, we can finally lay him to rest." he breathed. "Set's pyramid can actually have a use beyond the hardship and suffering of the humans."

But Isis shook her head firmly, "No, Thoth, we are going to put Osiris back together, and then he will take back the Pschent from Set and rule as pharaoh again."

"What do you mean, 'we'?" gasped the moon-god. "Isis, bringing people back from the dead is..."

"Not impossible, not forbidden." she cut across him. "No-one has ever tried, and no-one has ever said it cannot or should not be done.

Please, Thoth, help me bring back my husband, if not just for me, but for Egypt."

Thoth frowned, but his heart told him that it was the right choice. Nodding, he collected his long Was and followed Isis out into the night.

On the bank of the Nile, Isis had already built an altar, upon which lay the assembled pieces of Osiris under a black cloth. Taking a golden ladle, she scooped water from the river and held it, her hand quivering slightly, over the altar. Their eyes met, and Thoth began to chant, tracing various shapes in the air as he paced slowly in a wide circle around her. As he completed the circuit, Isis raised her eyes to the sky and cried in a great voice, "Come, oh the life-giving Nile, come and restore your pharaoh. He who summoned you to bring your waters to the land demands your service once again!" Hurling the water high in the air, she stepped back as it splashed down upon Osiris' body. Speaking in unison, she and Thoth began to pray, their hands held out to their sides at shoulder height, palms facing the star-strewn sky.

A wind blew from the north, whipping up funnels of dust that circled around them, not crossing the invisible barrier Thoth had conjured. Somewhere behind the wind, from the direction of the palace, voices echoed in their direction. Angry, scared, and confused, it was impossible to hear clearly as the wind sped up, the waters of the Nile foaming silver-white in the dark. The limbs on the altar were beginning to shake, as though some tremor from the ground ran through them. The incoherent voices from beyond the circle were getting nearer, but Thoth and Isis kept chanting. Then, something dropped from the sky like a falcon stooping to the kill. Insubstantial as smoke, Thoth thought he saw a face glance at him out of the air before it dove under the black cloth, making it ripple and flutter. The wind stopped, and the Nile settled to its usual, gentle lapping on the sh ore.

"What have you done?!" cried the voice of Set from beyond the circle. The hyena-headed god was not the only one who stood staring at them in the moonlight. Behind him were grouped many of the other gods, Anhur and Shu among them.

"We have righted a terrible wrong, Set." proclaimed Isis triumphantly. "Behold, the true Pharoah returns!"

Thoth span around to see that, indeed, the black cloth on the altar was shifting, rising, falling away. It slipped to the ground as what lay beneath it rose. Osiris, shaking slightly but moving with firm strength, sat up and swung his legs off the flat stone. His eyes were bright, his back straight, and he crossed his arms over his chest, hands touching his shoulders as he bowed mockingly to the other gods.

Set's eyes were narrowed with fury. "We shall see what Ra makes of this." he cried. "Such dark magic cannot be allowed!"

The Mandjet had scarcely graced the eastern-most horizon when Set sent word to Ra of what had occurred during the night. None of the gods had ever seen Ra so angry as he threw open the doors of the palace and stormed inside. The sun itself seemed to redden in the sky and its usual warmth was replaced by a burning heat that drove everyone into the shade. Isis, Osiris, and Thoth stood a little apart from the other gods, all of whom were whispering together, glancing over at them with a mixture of fear and confusion.

Angry as he was, Ra still listened carefully to everything Isis had to say: about the strange lions and their curious behavior, about her long search to the very edges of existence, and the final, mystical rite that had brought Osiris back into the world of the living. Set tried to speak, but Ra silenced him with a flash of his sharp eyes.

"What you have done challenges the very fabric of life, Isis." Ra said heavily. "Death is not the end, but simply the next stage. Even I will one day make my final voyage into the Duat. Osiris cannot be allowed a second life on this mortal plane."

Isis raised her hands to her mouth, and Thoth hung his head. "It was all for nothing." he thought sadly.

"However," continued Ra, and the three of them looked back up at him, hopeful and expectant. "The Duat needs a Pharoah, just as the mortal world does. Osiris will rule the ever-growing numbers of souls. It will be good for Anubis to have some company down there, too." He nodded at the black-skinned, jackal-headed god, whose face split into a wide smile. "It will not be an easy path, Osiris." Ra warned, "For even after my nightly battle, Apophis still hunts in the darkness, seeking to devour any soul that strays from the path of the Duat. You and Anubis must guard and guide them."

Osiris bowed his head. "Thank you, Lord of the Two Horizons. I shall do this with honor."

Tears were flowing down Isis' cheeks, but there was nothing to be done. So, she and Osiris shared one last night together, and then he entered the great, stone pyramid which the humans of the Black Land had finished building not long before. There, in the central chamber, he lay down in a sarcophagus, a great, bejeweled coffin, and breathed out his life spirit. The soul of Osiris rose up into the wind and joined Anubis as he traveled back into the Duat.

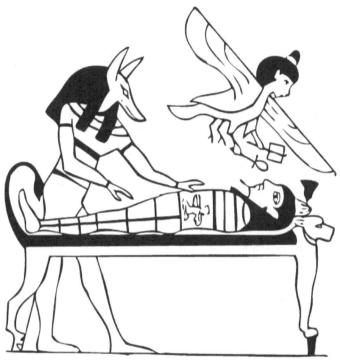

Anubis, the jackal-headed god of funerals and change

Chapter 6: The New Kingdom

There were many gods of Egypt, and all had their own duties and abilities. Sekhmet, the lioness-headed goddess whose jaws unleashed flame and brought sickness, was also an expert healer. Together with Ra, she battled to keep Apophis, the dreaded serpent of the Duat, at bay. Thoth, the god of the moon and of magic, had the delicate, long-beaked head of an ibis. He was among the wisest of the gods, with skilled hands and a subtle mind. The hyena-headed Set, god of deserts and storms, ruled Egypt as pharaoh after Osiris had been killed by lions only to be subsequently brought back to life and sent to rule over the Duat.

Set was about as cunning as it was possible to be. His arm was strong, and his temper terrible. When he was young he had forever been a trickster, delighting to play pranks on his brothers and sisters. But on becoming pharaoh, such was his power and authority that he did not bother to rule with attentiveness or prudence, trusting his guards and regional overseers to keep the people under control. The first great pyramid, in honor of Osiris, had been finished and now housed Osiris' body while his spirit ruled the land of the dead. Thus, it was that Set had commanded a new construction project: a huge statue of a sphinx, a monster with the head of a man and the body of a lion.

With Set's mind so focused on his own activities, it was easy for Isis, wife of Osiris, to keep secret that which would one day rock the foundations of Set's rule: she was pregnant. On the final night before Osiris went into the Duat to take up his rule, they had conceived a child. As the baby within her grew, she used her own powers to mask her condition, and before the time came to deliver, she took a boat down the Nile. With a full moon passing over the mighty river's delta, she gave birth to a boy: Horus. Like his grandfather Ra, Horus had the head of a falcon but with black hair rather than blue.

With the aid of her handmaidens, Isis raised Horus in secret, far from the spies and servants of Set. He grew to be strong of body and mind, with far-seeing eyes. On rising to manhood, he asked his mother about his father, where he was, and why he, Horus, had lived his whole life among the reeds and marshlands of the delta. Isis, knowing that she could not keep the truth from her son any longer, told of the death of Osiris, of her long search for his body, and finally of his fate: to leave the world of the living and rule the land of the dead.

"But why would lions behave like that?" asked Horus. "They live for the good of the pride. Such beasts would never separate and carry off their prey. It is almost as though they were bewitched."

Tears filled the eyes of his mother, hearing her own suspicions spoken aloud by her son.

Turning to her with a fierce expression, Horus proclaimed, "Mother, it is time for me to leave these flooded plains and take back my father's throne." And so, raising a sail on a small reed boat, Horus traveled up the Nile, his bright eyes unblinking, even as the sun rose up out of the east.

Every god was clustered in the council chambre of Set's great palace when the news came that Isis was returning. Joyous faces were struck with surprise when they saw her accompanied by her falcon-headed son. "Ra, Lord of the Two Horizons!" cried Anhur, the war-god. "You seem refreshed and whole. How have you done this?"

Horus stepped forward proudly. "I am not Ra who rides the Mandjet. I am Horus, son of Osiris, and I have returned to take what is mine by right: The throne and the Pschent of Egypt!"

With shocked murmurs echoing off the walls, all eyes turned to Set, who sat tall and erect in his throne. Never a coward, the hyena-headed pharaoh stood to face his young rival. "The challenge has been laid and accepted. I would not wish to spill the blood of a fellow god, and thus I propose a race: Tomorrow at noon we shall race boats made of stone from Abydos for a league upstream. Only he who is strong enough and blessed with the will of the Nile can be pharaoh." His eyes narrowed and his long tongue lolled out of his mouth as he grinned at the falcon-headed god. The other gods glanced at each other perplexedly: how could anyone sail a boat made from stone? But Horus did not blink as their eyes met. "Tomorrow at noon, then." he replied.

Hundreds of excited folk lined the banks of the Nile to watch the great race. Horus and Set were both in their small, grey boats, both of which seemed perilously close to sinking, made of stone as they were. Thoth and Anhur in a large boat constructed, as usual, from reeds, floated off to the side, marking the start line. "Three!" cried Anhur, "Two! One! Start!" With a roar from the crowd to push them forward, Set and Horus dextrously raised their sails and plied their oars to fight the gentle current of the Nile. Thoth and Anhur's boat, although larger than either of the racing craft, was lighter and kept pace easily. Children laughed as they ran along the bank, watching the two gods as they paddled feverishly. Set splashed Horus, sending more water into his boat and risking sinking it altogether, but Horus kept rowing, his powerful arms working with long, sure strokes.

The boats edged slowly on, and despite Set's best efforts, Horus was pulling ahead. Growling in frustration, Set heaved and sweated, desperately trying to close the gap, but Thoth and Anhur had already pulled ahead, waiting at the mark that was the finish line. A great cheer reverberated across the water as Anhur raised his hand, awarding the victory to Horus even as Set pulled up behind him.

They brought their boats to the shore, where the assembled gods were applauding and congratulating the young, falcon-headed god. Shaking with rage, Set ran to Horus' boat and cried, "Brothers and sisters, we have been deceived! Horus' boat was never made from stone!" To prove his point, he picked Horus' boat up out of the water and smashed it on the shore. Broken spars of wood and reeds splintered all over the place, revealing a thin layer of stones glued carefully onto a normal reed boat, hiding the yellow with grey.

There was a painful silence, during which all turned to Horus. But without a single ruffled feather, he calmly strode to Set's own craft and laying his hands on it, called, "Two can play at that game, Set!" Splitting the boat on a rock, he held it up to show the crowd: Just as Horus had covered a reed boat with small stones, so Set had covered his in thin layers of flint. The silence that followed this second revelation was deafening.

Then Thoth laughed. "The trickster has at last been beaten at his own game!" Laughter rippled among the gods and soon every one of them had tears rolling down their cheeks as they clapped their hands and slapped their thighs, while Set, seething with rage at his own trick being discovered, stared at them all, his knuckles white and shaking.

"I believe," said Horus, slowly and proudly as the noise died away, "That my victory stands."

Set took one look at him, then grabbed a spear from one of his guards. "Think again, you little, jumped-up, pigeon-headed thief!"

With a howl of rage, he threw himself at Horus, who did not dodge the spear thrust quickly enough. A searing pain shot through his head as Set's weapon skewered his eye, half-blinding him. But he was young and strong, and although the agony was terrible, greater was his rage. Even as Set drew back the spear to strike again, with a whistling, screeching cry, Horus seized the spear and wrenched it from Set's grip. Blood trickled down his feathered face as he whirled the weapon through the air, striking his foe first on the shoulder, then the hip, then the leg.

Great warrior though he was, there was nothing Set could do against this blistering onslaught. Horus' next thrust pushed him back fast. Pivoting on one foot, the hyena-headed god tried to dodge aside, but a shooting pain in his ankle was followed swiftly by the world being turned upside down as Horus knocked his leg out from under him. Small stars popped in front of his eyes as he landed heavily on the stony ground. He tried to get up, but the spear blade at his throat stopped him.

Horus was panting, not with exertion but with emotion. His single eye glared down at Set. "I am Pharoah now, Set." Horus hissed. "I believe that you conspired to kill my father and take his throne. But while I cannot prove this, I can at least do this: You are banished from the Black Land. Go back to the desert and weave your storms. I never want to see you again."

Plucking the red and white Pschent from Set's head, Horus removed the spear from his enemy's throat. No-one rose to Set's defense, and so he slunk away, obedient to his pharaoh's will. Thus it is that still storms come from the desert, sending sand over the fertile farmlands, ever-present reminders of the menace of Set, lord of the Red Land.

Chapter 7: Into the Duat

N eith couldn't remember falling over. She couldn't remember hitting her head. She knew that she lived in Abydos, that she was fifty-seven years old – a good age – that she had three children, the eldest of whom, Mika, was forever playing tricks on his younger sisters, even when he had grown up and had a family of his own. She remembered how hard it had been since her husband, Anees, had died. But she didn't remember how she came to be floating here, quieter than breath, lighter than smoke, watching her own lifeless body just lying there.

"I am dead." she told herself, but only scarcely believed it. She watched as though in a daze, as her children ran in, totally ignoring the Neith who floated next to them, trying to catch their attention to console them as tears flooded down their cheeks. Priests came, solemn men with shaven heads, and they bore her body away. Neith went with them, leaving no footprints on the soft earth. Time seemed to drift by strangely, leaping past in phases as the priests of Anubis, the jackal-headed god of funerals, prepared her body. She had to look away at this point as she couldn't bear to watch when they removed her organs and placed them carefully in beautifully decorated canopic jars. All except for the heart. The heart, she knew, was the seat of memory and emotion, of thought and power. She would need it at the end. The priests wrapped her body in resin-soaked bandages, chanting all the while, sometimes placing small semi-precious stones or scraps of parchment covered in spells in amongst the bandages. The final, most important item was the scarab broach, directly over her heart.

"I'm really going!" she said, although none of the men heard her. "I can't believe I actually have the chance to pass through the Duat." That was the fear of every normal man and woman: that only pharaohs, direct descendants of mighty Horus, died and made the journey into the Duat. They worried that their souls would simply dissipate into nothingness, like ashes on the wind. As time leaped forward once again, Neith sensed rather than felt a change. Looking down, she saw that on her own translucent chest, there now crawled a bright blue scarab beetle, just like the one that adorned her body before her. The beetle scuttled around in a circle before resting gently above her heart. It was time.

A gust of wind seemed to pass through the chamber, and Nieth was floating upwards. Glancing down, she saw her own body being carried towards a small tomb, little more than a hole in the rockface, not far from where she had placed her own dear husband's body. But already, the town of Abydos was shrinking beneath her as she soared high into the sky, joining a current of higher air that rushed her toward the setting sun. Ahead, she could just see the form of a great reed boat cruising through the darkening sky, on which stood two figures: one with the head of a lioness, the other a falcon. "Sekhmet and Ra!" she gasped, averting her eyes in fear. But the two gods did not seem to notice her. An unheard scream escaped Neith's lips as the horizon zoomed toward her. Then all was blackness.

As Neith's eyes became accustomed to the dark, she felt something soft pass against her leg. Leaping away, she stared down to see two golden eyes watching her. A faint mewing came to her ears, and now she could discern the cat's sinuous outline. Breathing a sigh of relief, she took in her surroundings. Cats were the guardians of the underworld, she knew; maybe this one had come to guide her. She felt in the pockets of her robe and found the heavy scroll she had hoped to find. "The Book of the Dead." she murmured, opening the scroll and trying to read the many different spells and clues the priests had prepared. "Not that any of them can really know what to expect here!" she scoffed.

Neith saw now that the hall in which she found herself was vast, with no visible light sources. Out of the night that surrounded her, she could hear a faint noise, as though a giant snake was slithering over dry leaves. "Apophis!" she breathed, "The Eater of Souls." She stared around her, trying to step as quietly as she could, but the sound had disappeared the moment she had become aware of it. On she walked, her feline companion sometimes appearing to her left, sometimes to her right. The outlines of three tall doors loomed before her. There was no visible wall between them, but Neith knew that she could not pass by them: the only way forward was through.

"Which one do I take?" She glanced down at the cat, but it just sat and licked a paw unconcernedly.

Taking a deep breath, Neith pushed open the righthand door and stepped boldly through into fire. Neith shrieked and tried to go back, but the doorway had disappeared. There was no way out but forward, so she ran, hands over her head, choking with the smoke. Another set of doors appeared before her, and she hurled herself through the central one. The cool darkness of the floor beyond was an embrace so sweet she nearly cried. The cat, seemingly unperturbed by what had just happened, stretched and yawned as though wondering what was taking her so long. Limbs trembling, Neith tried to stand, but a vibration through the floor told her that she wasn't alone. Heart pounding, mouth dry, she raised her head ever so slowly to see what lay before her. What she saw made her nearly pass out.

A giant serpent with vicious red eyes and vivid green scales was slithering slowly across the hall. Its long, forked tongue tasted her scent on the air, and Apophis raised his dead, eyes flashing excitedly. Frozen in terror, Neith could do nothing but watch the dread creature as it bared down on her. Then, a spear flew down from above and struck the snake in the side. Apophis, hissing with rage, turned to face its attacker. Finding her feet, Neith ran as two giant figures leaped down from a waiting reed boat, spears in hand. Ra and Sekhmet lunged and dodged, but Neith didn't stop to see what happened as another trio of doors appeared before her. She dived through the lefthand one, but there was no floor beyond.

She was falling. Falling. Air was whipping her face. Darkness was rushing up to meet her. Then she slammed into the ground. It took a few moments for her to recover her senses, or it might have been hours or even days. "Who can tell in this endless dark?" she wondered. Rising to her knees, she saw another hallway before her, but this time there stood a crowd of people, shadowy and strangely insubstantial. With a shudder, she realized that while none of these silent figures had faces, they were all certainly watching her. A voice echoed down the hall, "This is the hall of Maat. Speak your truth." Drawing her scroll out, Neith read the vague description of the hall of Maat and guessed what she had to do.

Approaching the first figure, she looked up into its shapeless face and said, "I have never killed anyone." The figure nodded and walked past her, disappearing into the darkness. To the next figure, she said, "I have never cheated at dice." Again, this was true, and the figure passed her by. But there was still a crowd to convince of her sinless life. Each time a faceless entity turned to her, she had to state another sin she had not committed.

After a while, however, Neith was running out of sins, and there were still a handful of assessor spirits to face. But this was why the priests of Anubis had given her the scarab broach. On the underside of the scarab, it was carefully written, "Do not stand as a witness against me." This spell stopped her heart, which could not lie, from giving away the truth. Thus, Neith proclaimed that she had never eavesdropped, although what mother hadn't listened at her child's door to hear when they would next try to sneak out of the house?

She promised that she had never stolen bread, which was true, but she had borrowed some flour from her neighbor without asking.

God Anubis & Thoth with scales pair, Weighing of Heart, the afterlife ritual in Duat.

Finally, the way ahead was clear, and ahead, she could see a tall figure with black skin and the head of a jackal. The scarab on her chest seemed to shake with terror as she approached Anubis, next to whom stood a large set of scales. Beside him sat Amet, a monstrous creature with the head of a crocodile and the body of a hippo. This, Neith knew, was the final test: Reaching to her chest, she brushed the scarab aside and, her mouth dry, reached within her own body and brought out her heart. Anubis took the heart without a word and set it on the scales, drawing a pure white ostrich feather from a pocket and placing it on the other side of the scales. Hardly daring to breathe, Neith watched as the beam vibrated, sensing and judging her heart. If her life had been truly impure, it would sink to the ground, and Amet would leap forward to devour it and her.

With a whisp and a clink, the ostrich feather sank. Anubis smiled at her. "Your heart is true, Neith, daughter of Alin. My lord Osiris awaits you." He bowed his head and motioned for her to pass him by. Ahead, a golden light seemed now to illuminate the far end of the hall. Neith almost skipped with joy as she collected her heart and walked toward the light. There, on a beautiful golden throne, sat tall, noble Osiris, god of the underworld. In his hands he held a crook and a flail, and his smile was warm as he welcomed her into his presence. Neith bowed, the cat slinking around her legs, rubbing against them with a happy purr.

Motioning to his right, Osiris held back a curtain beyond which there was no more hall, no dark monsters, nor burning fire. An endless field rose and fell into the distance; golden reeds swayed in a light breeze. Tears of joy rolled down Neith's cheeks as she saw three people she recognized: her mother, father, and dear husband Anees. They were busy with the harvest, but no ache nor sweat troubled them, and they straightened to wave at her as she stepped through the curtain into the warm light of the Duat's Field of Reeds.

Part II: Mesopotamia

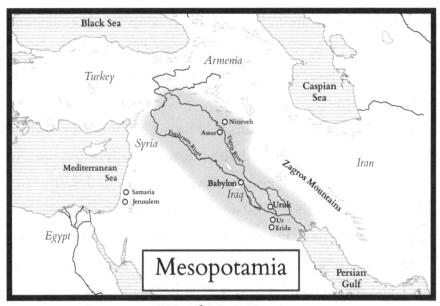

Map of Mesopotamia

Chapter 1: Atra-Hasis

In the beginning, we are told there were three gods. None of them shared where they came from or how, only that they were there first. Arching high above the others was Anu, the sky god. Standing like a mountain in a storm was Enlil, the earth god. Rushing here, there, and everywhere was Enki, the god of fresh water that brings life. The world was wide and lush, with bright streams and dark woods and high hills and vast stretches of steppe and plain. Together the gods made the dingir, lesser immortals who worked the fields, herded the animals, and stitched the clothes.

But the hearts of the dingir grew dissatisfied. One among them, a clever and resourceful dingir called Geshtu voiced his anger, speaking out among his fellows. "Just as the three above us live forever, so do we. We will not fade into the earth like the deer of the plains nor the larks in the sky. Why should we work in the blazing sun while Anu and Enlil and Enki watch and feast?" Many heard his words and too voiced their anger. Taking up weapons that they had to defend the herds from the wolves, Geshtu led them against the three.

Enki wanted to listen, but Enlil, whose rage was always ready to shake the ground, struck Geshtu hard on the head, striking him to the ground. He moved no more. The other dingir backed away, now afraid for their own lives, but Anu held Enlil back, saying, "Wait brother. Do not shed more blood this day. Geshtu riled their hearts and now he lies quiet."

Enki, too, stepped forward. "It is hard for the dingir, immortals as they too are, to work for their food as hard while we sit by, exhausted though we are from our labors." He waved around at the wide, beautiful lands. "Let us have another race come forth. They shall ease the dingirs' burdens some."

Enlil frowned but nodded his assent, and Anu called out to one of the dingir, a woman called Ninhursag. "You who delight to work with clay, take the body of your brother, Geshtu, and make a race that shall aid you henceforth."

Ninhursag bowed and began her work. First, she ground up the bones of Geshtu, mixing his blood and flesh with clay from the ground. Then she called on all the dingir and the three to spit into the mixture. Now ready, she took a great spinning potter's wheel, with which she had often made beautiful bowls and cups, and threw the clay onto it. Splitting the clay into fourteen, she fashioned as many wombs, which she laid in the sun under a beautiful boxwood tree, seven upon the left and seven upon the right.

The sun rose and set for ten months, and Ninhursag came back to the spot to find the first fourteen humans crawling out of their wombs. She welcomed them into the world, and Anu, Enlil, and

Enki smiled upon them, for they were fine and strong. The humans learned much from the dingir: when it was time to sew and to reap, how to help a mother cow give birth, which berries were good, and which trees had the best wood for making bows. In time, they became as many as the birds in the trees and the fish in the rivers.

As humanity multiplied, they found that they needed more space, and so sought out new places, traveling in families and tribes widely across the plains and steppes of this lush land. There was one man among them who was wise and kind, a strong leader and a good husband. His name was Atra-Hasis, and when the old leader of his tribe died, many among his friends persuaded him to lead the council. But while Atra-Hasis led his people with good sense and purpose, there were many others who were not as thoughtful. They chopped down trees they did not need; they left rubbish lying by the rivers. They did not honor the deer they hunted by using all the pieces, as the dingir had taught them, so that nothing was wasted.

Enlil, the earth god, watched these men and women who dishonored the good things around them with mounting disquiet, and decided in his heart that the time had come for a fresh start. "Anu!" he called one day, striding up a mountain to where the sky god sat and watched his clouds waft lazily along the breeze. "The humans are dishonorable and wasteful, and arrogant as well! We must wash the world clean of them and begin again." Anu frowned, and to their right, a splashing of water could be heard as Enki, the god of fresh water which brings life, came to join them in council.

"I disagree, brother Enlil." he replied. "Some are still good and follow the dingirs' teachings well."

"Perhaps," spat Enlil, "but if a tree is infested by termites, it will fall on its own, even if some of those termites only eat as much as they need and no more. Once the tree falls, the termites will continue to eat until the forest is gone."

Anu nodded, glancing from one brother to the other. "We shall send a flood." he decided, being rewarded with a broad smile from Enlil. "It shall take a week to prepare. But you, brother Enki, must not tell the humans what is coming. Do you swear?"

Enki could not ignore a request from his own brother and so swore. But the next day, he went down to where Atra-Hasis, who he knew to be a good man, was collecting fish from a trap in the river. Enki noted with approval that the man took a variety of fish, not just the big but also the small ones, releasing the rest. "Why do you not take only the big fish?" The god asked, knowing the answer already.

Atra-Hasis, seeing the shining reeds of the god's cloak, realized who was watching him and bowed low. "I like a big fish on my plate as much as the next man, oh lord of the clear water, but if I take all of them, then my children and their children after them will have none, only the small fish."

Enki nodded. "Take down your houses and build a boat, Atra-Hasis."

The man stared at him in confusion, for the river by which they lived was not large, and the sea was far away. "Why?"

But the god shook his head. "Because I told you to. The work must be done in seven days. Do not ask any more of me." And with that he left the man standing by the river, a basket of fish under his arm.

Atra-Hasis did not wait to consider the cryptic orders. A god had told him to do something, and that was enough for him. Returning to his village, he gave the orders. Such was the trust that his people had in him, that they did as he asked without question, and so they worked, demolishing their homes one by one, and using the timber to construct a wide-beamed boat. It took many days, for Atra-Hasis sensed that the boat must be big enough to hold them all, and he would not leave one man behind. On the seventh day, they herded their sheep and goats aboard, loaded the last of their supplies, and w aited.

Looking up into the sky where he knew dwelt Anu, Atra-Hasis saw the darkest clouds he had ever seen looming above them. A drop of rain struck him on the forehead, and soon the deluge came. The river rose and broke its banks, spreading wide over the flat valley. And still the waters came. From the north, up the valley, came a rushing and a splintering of trees. All stared in horror as a mighty wave poured down the valley, and the timbers that had held the boat steady were washed away as the craft was lifted up upon the flood waters.

For many days and nights, they floated on the terrible tide. Then, one day, Atra-Hasis was woken by his son, shaking him excitedly awake. "I can see the tops of trees, father!" he cried happily. And Atra-Hasis saw that he was right. Another day passed, and they felt the keel of the boat grind against a stone. They had been carried into a new valley, and the people rushed out of the boat to kneel in the wet grass and cry happily. Atra-Hasis ordered his people to gather around while he built a fire and sacrificed his best ram to the gods, thanking them for their safe deliverance from the flood.

High above a mountain peak, Enlil raged and pounded the rocks, "You betrayed our secret, brother! You told that human of the danger!" but Anu held him back.

"Rest assured, brother," smiled Enki, "I did not break my silence on the flood. I simply told Atra-Hasis to build a boat."

"Besides, do you not taste the smoke on the wind, brother?" Anu asked him. "These people are grateful and good. They honor us fitly. Perhaps there is hope for mankind after all."

Chapter 2: Adapa's Choices

It had been many years since the great flood had come. So many, in fact, that the old grey beards had been barely babes in their mothers' arms at the time. Atra-Hasis had long since died, and his son's son now ruled a well-built town called Eridu. Other towns and villages had been founded in the lands around, and while there came no sign from the gods of further displeasure, the people of Eridu felt a vague uncertainty, a disquiet in their hearts even as they went about their daily business.

Many went to the priest of Enki, a man called Adapa, for guidance, for it was still well remembered that Enki had aided mankind in surviving the flood. Adapa was counted among the wise of Eridu, even if his beard was still not grey. But even he could not guide the people in their doubt too well. "If the gods have a message for us, they will make their feelings known." He tried to reassure those who came to him, but this rarely seemed to help. He even asked the dingir, the lesser gods who still roamed the land at times, speaking to humans when they wished. But they had no answer for him. Some patted him kindly on the shoulder but then moved on, some laughed at his perplexity for he was just a man.

There came a day when Adapa was out on the great river, fishing. All of a sudden, a mocking cry came up out of the sky, followed by a gust of wind so strong that his small craft flipped over, sending the priest headfirst into the water. Swimming to the shore, Adapa found himself looking at a strange, winged dingir he had never seen before. "Who are you, dingir?" he said reverently. The dingir cackled, "Isimud am I, the wind from the south."

"And why, great Isimud, did you see fit to sink my boat?"

Isimud spun around in a circle, laughing, "Isimud was bored. Isimud thought the holy man needed a bath! Haha!"

Some of the frustration that had been building in Adapa's mind, unbeknownst to even him, came forth. Time seemed to stand still for a moment as he regarded Isimud and his lop-sided smile. He could just walk away, but somehow he knew he couldn't. "Dingir or not," he bellowed, "I shall teach you to smite without cause." Throwing himself at the surprised dingir, Adapa seized the south wind's wings and swung him around. A terrible crack shot through the air and Isimud screamed. Twisting out of the priest's grip, the dingir tried to rise into the air, but one of his wings was broken. "Isimud will tell the others of this!" Cried the enraged, injured lesser god. "Isimud will! Isimud will!" And he disappeared in a gust of wind.

That night, Adapa lay in bed, his mind racing. Every time he closed his eyes, a terrible image of Anu himself, the god of the sky and master of the winds, came to him. Finally, he could not fight sleep any longer, and he allowed his eyelids to droop. High up in the sky, Anu frowned down on the man. "What gives you the right to strike a dingir, mortal?" He boomed. Adapa tried to explain, but somehow the words kept getting jumbled in his mouth. His arms and legs felt as though they were trapped in deep water, so that every movement was sluggish. Then Enki, god of fresh water that brings life, appeared.

"Brother, let this man, my priest, do a penance for his act."

With Anu's permission, Enki instructed Adapa. "You must gain the sympathy of those who guard the gates of heaven: Tammuz and Gishzida. If you are successful, they will offer you hospitality: food, drink, and fresh clothes, but food and drink of the gods may prove dangerous for you, so accept only the fresh clothing."

The priest was still nodded fervently as the cock outside his window crowed.

Everyone knew where the gates of heaven were, but few had ever been in sight of them and lived to tell the tale. But Enki had given Adapa an order, and the priest dared not risk the gods' wrath further. So, he left Eridu and headed towards the high mountains that arched all the way from the east, round to the north, and, it was said, continued far on into the west. The gate lay atop one of the highest mountains in that range, and although it took many weeks of tiring travel, finally the priest came near to the cloud-wreathed slopes that led like a stair up into the sky.

Enki had told Adapa that he must gain the sympathy of the two dingir who guarded the gates of heaven, and so the priest took mud and smeared it in his hair and beard. Then, he ripped his clothes and rolled himself in the dirt, all to make himself look like a man in mourning for some passed loved one. Thus prepared, he continued on up through the soft dampness of the clouds. The wind whipped at his face and hands, and then the clouds parted to reveal the summit, at which stood two great stones, standing vertically. Atop them lay a third horizontal stone so that a doorway in the sky stood at the highest point of the world.

Before the doorway, there stood two tall dingir. Swallowing hard, for his mouth was dry, Adapa approached the two. "Hail, Tammuz and Gishzida, grand guardians of the gates." He called. "I am Adapa, priest of Enki in Eridu." The two of them stared down at him, clearly surprised.

"Greetings, Adapa." Replied Tammuz, who stood taller than his companion. "What brings you to us?" He eyed the man's torn clothes and dirty face. "Particularly now, as you are clearly in mourning for someone close to you?"

Adapa hid his pleasure at the success of his deceit. "I am here at the order of my lord Enki, god of fresh water that brings life."

The two dingir nodded. "We shall fetch the mighty Enki for you, but in the meantime will you sit and eat with us?" Gishzida reached into his bag and held out some bread and a flask. But Adapa remembered the warning of Enki.

"Thank you, great-hearted Gishzida, but I dare not eat the food of the gods, for I am but a man."

"Are you sure?" The dingir offered the food again. "This is the bread of life and the wine of immortality."

A sudden urge to accept flared in Adapa's mind, but again the words of Enki came to him: "Food and drink of the gods may prove dangerous for you." And so again he refused politely.

Tammuz stepped forward now. "Let us at least offer you a cloak. It is cold up here, even for dingir, and your clothes have seen better days." Reaching into his own bag, the guardian handed Adapa a warm cloak, which he accepted gratefully.

Then, between the mighty stone doorposts, there came Anu and Enki as though they had been expecting him to arrive at this very moment, and they looked down on the priest with interest.

"Why did you refuse the food and drink, priest Adapa?" Asked Anu.

Adapa glanced at Enki, "My lord Enki instructed me not to eat of the gods' food or drink their drink."

Anu laughed. "What ill has he brought on mankind?" He glanced at his brother Enki, who smiled sadly. "Perhaps it is better this way. Who really wants to live forever anyway? Your penance is complete, wise Adapa. Your home calls you." With a wave of his hand, Anu summoned a breeze that lifted the priest gently and bore him away as swiftly as a bird on the wing.

Returning to Eridu, Adapa found another man, Torin the miller, waiting for him. "Priest of Enki," the man bobbed his head respectfully, "I come for guidance: I wish to build a great water wheel to help grind grain faster, now that the new farmsteads to the north are thriving. But will the river rise again and flood?"

Adapa looked at the man for a moment, and then a strange surety filled his mind. He thought about the long journey he had just made, starting with that mad fight with the dingir Isimud. He had acted without thinking, and while that could have spelled doom for him, instead he had been sent on an incredible adventure. He realized then how close he had been to gaining immortality. If he had just disobeyed Enki's instructions, he could have lived forever. But he did not regret his choice. On the contrary, he realized that he had been taught a valuable lesson.

Smiling, he held Torin firmly by the shoulders, looking him straight in the eyes. "We worry about our lives and what will come next. We wonder if there is a greater purpose to be had. But life has its own purpose. The mighty oak is happy to sway in the wind and let its leaves fall and grow and fall again. Do not fear what is to come; expect it with patience and hope. No man lies on his deathbed regretting taking risks. Build your water wheel, and good luck to you!"

Chapter 3: The Kindness of Simurgh

F ar to the north stood a mighty mountain known as the Hara Berezaiti, or "High Watchpost" in a primeval tongue of men. From here, we are told, came all waters for every river. Near the summit, there was a cave, where dwelled perhaps the greatest bird ever to grace the back of the winds. The Simurgh was ancient and gigantic, strong enough to bear an elephant in its talons, which were like those of a lion. Her head was that of a dog, and her feathers shone like copper. Though she was fearsome to behold, the Simurgh was a kindly creature who knew every language of men as well as many truths of the world.

In the wide lands beyond the Tigris and the Euphrates there now lived many different peoples, for the terrible flood was now a legend to be told around the fireside in the evening. Among these many cities and tribes, there was a king called Saam. On the day of his son's birth, he rushed into the chamber of his wife to be greeted by the sound of wailing. With his heart in his mouth, Saam approached the bed of his dear partner in life, Leila. "What is it, light of my eyes?" The king could not keep his voice from trembling. "Has the child died ?"

Leila shook her head but held the boy out to show him. "I do not know what message this sends from the gods, husband." She whispered.

And so, Saam, seasoned warrior though he was, stepped back in shock and confusion, for the boy had white hair and white skin, and his eyes were red. There had been tales, told to him by his grandfather, of a terrible albino lion called Zal – an ancient term for "white" – that had caused great destruction in the long past, and these stories whirled around Saam's mind even as his own son wriggled in his mother's arms. But he had not become king through avoiding the hard choices, even as this one made him weep. "He is Zal." The king proclaimed. "He is a danger to us all. He shall be left on the High Watchpost, the holy mountain which sends us water, and the gods shall decide his fate."

Thus Zal, though barely a few days old, was left on the foothills of Hara Berezaiti, even as he wailed for his mother. High amongst the pure white clouds, the Simurgh bent her ears to the breeze and listened. She had had little experience with mankind in her long years but knew the sound of a young creature in need. Spreading her wings wide, the Simurgh leaped onto the wind and soared down, following the plaintive cries, her feathers brushing the tops of the trees.

On finding the pure white baby, the great bird realized at once what must have happened. "You have been proclaimed Zal, little one." She said, nuzzling the now giggling infant with her nose. "But you shall take this name they have forced on you as your own. Come, little Zal." With a gentle caress, the Simurgh brought the baby up to her cave on the summit of the high mountain and raised him as her own. As Zal grew older, he would ride on her back as she flew high above the world, telling him of the many lands and peoples below them. He was a patient and eager learner and listened to everything that the wise old bird had to tell him.

As Zal grew to adulthood, however, he yearned to re-join the world of men. The Simurgh was greatly saddened by this but knew she could not stop him and loved him too much to try. Therefore, on his last night before his journey down the mountain, she gave him three golden feathers from her wing. "If ever you have need of my guidance again," she said, "throw one of these into the fire and I shall come." The young, white-haired man hugged her in gratitude, not just for the feathers, but for all her kindness throughout his life.

Following a river down into the lands to the south of the mountain on which he had lived his entire life, Zal came to a small village, where some of the villagers shouted at him, fearing him to be a demon. Others, however, when he did not attack them, welcomed him into their homes. But Zal did not want to stay in one place. His entire life had been spent always returning to the cave at the summit of Hara Berezaiti, and although he had seen much of the world from above, he now wanted to travel even further. Therefore, when a trading caravan, led by a thick-necked man called Bazim passed by the village, he left with them as a guard, for there were many bandits plaguing the roads at that time.

The first city they came to was Kabol, around which stood mighty walls with many towers. Although he had seen such places from the sky, Zal was awed at the sheer number of folk, jostling each other, shouting, vendors selling their wares and traders pushing through the market while children ran here and there laughing. As thick as the press of people was, many stepped out of the way as the tall, startlingly white figure of Zal came through, wary eyes glancing up at his pale face and strange, red eyes.

Then, a number of horsemen urged their horses through the city gates behind Bazim's party, leading a procession in the center of which rode a man with a golden circlet about his brows. Behind him came a beautiful young woman who, judging from their similar noses and sharp eyes, had to be his daughter. The crowd parted and Bazim pulled Zal over to the side as the royal party trooped past. Pale as he was surrounded by so many tanned faces, the princess' eyes were drawn to him, and within his chest Zal felt a strange lifting sensation, as though his heart had grown wings and was trying to escape. "Keep your eyes to yourself!" Hissed the trader in his ear. "That's the princess Rudaba, and king Mehrab won't take kindly to anyone staring at her like you are now!" Zal nodded, but still, he could not tear his eyes away from the retreating back of the royal procession. Rudaba's dark hair fell like a waterfall of the deepest night down her back, and he watched as long as he could until she had disappeared up the street.

That night, while Bazim and the other caravan guards played dice and drank in one of the many taverns in the town, Zal, disguising his white hair and skin with a thick cloak and hood, stole into the great palace of Mehrab. As though some god was guiding him, he found his way to the princess' chamber and crept inside. Rudaba was sitting by a window, gazing out into the starry sky. A sheaf of parchment lay on her lap. On hearing him enter, she did not cry out in fear or surprise but smiled at him as he removed his hood. "I knew you would come. When I saw you in the market today, I knew that tonight would be the night." Smiling more broadly at Zal's puzzled face, she continued. "I dreamt of you more than once, ever since I was a little girl." Raising the leaves of parchment, she showed him a number of drawings she had made, all of which showed Zal's face at different points in his young life.

"What magic is this?" He breathed, holding one of the pictures with shaking hands. Rudaba shrugged. "Who can say? But my father will never approve of you. If we are to go, we must go now." It took a moment for Zal to understand what she was saying, and then he nodded. Drawing one of the Simurgh's golden feathers from his tunic, he cast it into the fire and then turned to the window. It did not take long before the mighty wingbeats of the great, ancient bird were to be heard, and Zal and Rudaba, her eyes wide with astonishment, climbed carefully out of the window onto the Simurgh's broad back. "Where should I take you, dearest Zal?" She asked him.

"To a place which has never heard of Mehrab." Replied Zal. "A place where we can live in peace."

The Simurgh had taken the young couple far away from Kabol, over the mountains and back, as luck would have it, into the realm where Zal's father still ruled. But Zal had no desire to see the man who had cast him out, and so he and Rudaba built themselves a small cabin in the woods and lived a peaceful life as they had both wished. It came to pass that Rudaba became pregnant, and both were thrilled and excited to bring a new life into the world. But when the day came for the child to be born, Zal's wife was overcome with pain. No matter what they tried, the child would not come out. Fearing for her life and for the life of their unborn child, Zal placed the second feather in the fire, and soon the Simurgh alighted before their cabin, tucking her wings tightly against her body so that she could look in the window.

One look at Rudaba's pained, sweat-covered face was enough for the wise bird. "The child will not be born as one would hope." She said to a nervous Zal. "You must cut her open and bring the child out that way." Zal's jaw dropped.

"But that will kill my wife!" He cried.

"Not if you follow my instructions." Replied the Simurgh calmly, a small smile flashing through her eyes. Thus, with careful encouragement from his foster mother, Zal carefully sliced open his wife's belly, and pulled the screaming infant, a strong young boy, into the light. While the Simurgh hushed the new-born infant, Zal sewed the cut in Rudaba's belly closed.

Holding her now happily suckling son to her, Zal's wife wept with grateful tears as her husband thanked the Simurgh before she took flight again. Returning to his family, Zal took out the last golden feather and handed it to his son, who squeaked and immediately began sucking on it. "This last feather is for you, Rostam." He said, smiling into Rudaba's eyes. "The Simurgh has been so kind to me for my entire life, but such a gift is best shared with those I love the mo st."

Chapter 4: Gilgamesh and Enkidu

As the wind rippled the heads of corn, barley, and flax in dry, golden waves, it brought the scent of the new crop gently to the king's nostrils. Gilgamesh, high king of Uruk, strode around the steps of the great Ziggurat, the stepped pyramid-like temple to the sky-god, Anu. Behind him scuttled his councilors and a number of scribes. A tall, broad-shouldered man with long, thick beard which, like his carefully curled hair, shone as like the sands of the deserts far beyond the mighty river Euphrates, Gilgamesh liked visiting his building projects. This latest would be his greatest thus far, and he had more in mind. Ever since he had overthrown the previous king, Aga, Gilgamesh had been striving to rewrite not only the history of the Sumerian kingdom, but also the landscape. He had conquered new lands and new peoples; he had built great walls around Uruk and new roads, and now this great temple to Anu.

Hanging gardens of Babylon; Ziggurat

Some said that Gilgamesh was descended from the gods, that he was two-thirds god and one-third man. He snorted into his beard when he heard this, for it was mathematical nonsense, but few could deny that his powerful, imposing figure, his handsome face, not to mention his great victories in battle, were unparalleled. Kings of mighty cities had already bowed before him. He had brought civilization to an uncivilized world, and the mighty spears of his armies would soon march further north.

A shout brought Gilgamesh's mind away from thoughts of conquest starkly into the present moment. A great block of stone crashed past, barely a yard from him, to cries of fright and shock from his entourage. Apparently unfazed, the king stared up the steps from whence the stone had come, and saw a mason, pale as death, eyes bulging with terror. The royal guards were already leaping up to seize the man, and within moments he was cowering before the king.

"Mesh-he!" Gilgamesh summoned the man in charge of the building works. "Is this man married? Does he have children?"

Mesh-he glanced at the mason for a moment, then nodded. "Yes, my king." The day was hot, but it was not just heat which made him sweat.

"This man shall have thirty lashes of the whip each day, starting now. All shall watch and see the price of carelessness. I will see his wife; if she is pretty, she shall serve my chambers. His children are now slaves."

Without a further glance at the man, Gilgamesh swept past, a cruel smile twisting his lips. He enjoyed dealing out punishment nearly as much as riding his chariot into battle. Just as a spear thrust, judgment should be swift and decisive. "Forgiveness is for the weak!" He declared.

"Yes, my king." Mesh-he bowed, and the other viziers all nodded and followed suit.

Pointing at the road that led back to the city, Gilgamesh frowned. "That road must be wider, with new paving stones. The road to the temple cannot be a dirt track."

Again, Mesh-he bowed, "An inspired thought, my king." Gilgamesh paid even less heed to the expected flattery than if a soft breeze had ruffled his beard.

Behind the royal party, the mason, a man called Parum, was already being tied to a pole, his tunic having been torn from him to bare his back to the whip. Raising his eyes to the heavens, Parum began to pray for strength. As each lash sliced pain through him, he cried aloud to Anu, the sky-god, and to Ki, the earth-goddess. His voice could no longer be understood through the cries of pain, but high above him, in the ether between humanity and the vault of heaven, Anu heard not just Parum but a thousand others, all crying, whether with their tongues or in their hearts. Gilgamesh was a cruel king, but so were so many other humans. "I shall make an example of him." decided Anu, and sent a messenger, though the man he sent had no idea he was being sent or that he was, indeed, a messenger at all. The man Anu sent into the path of Gilgamesh, the mighty king of kings, was a poor man called Enkidu.

From the wilds he came, Enkidu, son of some forgotten man. He was a wanderer, wrapped in skins sewn together with thick thread made from hide. His feet, legs, arms, and hands were bare, tough, dark with sun and dust. His dark hair and beard were long and matted. He was as tall as Gilgamesh, but thin, for life in the wilderness is not an easy one. It came to pass that on the same day that Gilgamesh was out hunting with a few guards, Enkidu was wandering through the same patch of woodland. Gilgamesh wielded a great spear in his hands, with a wickedly sharp point that flashed in the early morning sun; Enkidu had only a rough staff, little more than a branch from a tree, stripped of leaves.

The king and his men had been hunting the bear for hours, having started in the grey wolf-light of the morning. Now they were following a rough track made by centuries of deer passing through the forest. It provided the easiest route through the trees and would decrease the likelihood of the bear hearing them. Gilgamesh guessed, from a pawprint they had found not long before, that the bear was heading to the lake beyond the forest to drink. A rustling of leaves up ahead made him stop and signal to his guards to halt. He leveled his spear, ready to strike, when a wild man appeared, coming in the opposite direction. Gilgamesh grunted his annoyance but raised his spear. "Out of the way, we are hunting."

"And I am walking." Replied the man, stopping a dozen paces or so from the king's party. He did not step aside.

Raising his eyes at his guards, Gilgamesh laughed. "We were looking for a mighty bear, and we have found a wretched, stinking hyena."

The man rolled his eyes. "If you can't tell the difference between a man and a hyena, I don't recommend hunting a bear. He is a mighty beast and will not suffer fools lightly."

Gilgamesh growled. "I am the king, you filthy creature. Gilgamesh, lord of all these lands."

"I am Enkidu." Replied the man. "How can you be king of land? The land belongs to Ki, just as the sky to Anu, and everything in between is free to go where it wishes."

The king stared at the man. "I have conquered all the lands and peoples between the great river Euphrates and the high mountains in the east."

"You alone?" Asked Enkidu, puzzled.

"My armies." Snapped Gilgamesh, wondering why he didn't just run this wild man through with his spear and carry on. "Well, they never conquered me." Said Enkidu. "And I've never met you before."

Finally, Gilgamesh's temper spoke, and he leveled his spear again. "Then die knowing that you have met the high king Gilgamesh!" He charged at Enkidu, aiming to bury the shining bronze blade deep in the man's chest, but the thick staff in the wild man's hands tapped the spear aside and knocked Gilgamesh lightly on the back, sending him flying past. A cry of rage from the guards was silenced by the king's equally furious roar as he span round, "Leave him; he is mine!" The spear blade arced through the air with a hiss to chop down upon the wild man's neck, but Enkidu dropped his staff and caught the spear shaft. The two men wrestled with each other, both gripping the spear with two hands, eyes blazing, teeth bared.

For what seemed hours they fought, the guards staring in amazement as the mighty king strove to overcome this pelt-wrapped wanderer. Finally, they both collapsed, the spear falling in between them. Both were covered in sweat, panting and shaking with exhaustion.

"You could have just let me pass." Grunted Enkidu.

"I am the king; all should bow before me!" Panted Gilgamesh.

"If I had bowed, you couldn't have got past me on this narrow path." Replied the wild man, wiping sweat from his brow.

A strange feeling started to inch up Gilgamesh's throat, within seconds he was laughing, tears falling down his cheeks.

"True!" He chuckled. "Guards!"

Behind him, the guards, who had sat down to watch the seemingly endless battle, leaped to their feet again.

"We shall go home. The bear is long gone, and I have a better prize."

The men glanced at each other, confused.

"Come with me, Enkidu." Said Gilgamesh, standing and offering the man his hand. "I have many advisors, but all of them tell me that I am right. I need someone who will tell me when I am wrong."

Enkidu looked long and hard at him, then accepted the king's help as he got to his feet.

High above, beneath the vault of heaven, Anu watched as the first step in Gilgamesh's journey took place. "The high king has made a friend." He said to himself, "And they shall do glorious things together."

Chapter 5: Gilgamesh and the Guardian of the Cedar Forest

Beyond the lands of Uruk and its neighboring cities lay a great range of mountains called the Zagros. None living knew whence this name came, but all knew that they were dangerous, full of treacherous slopes, dark forests, and ferocious beasts. Deep in one forest, full of cedar trees of great girth and majesty, lived an ogre called Humbaba. He claimed that Enlil, the god of the earth, had placed him there as the forest's guardian, and he ruled with an iron will and a strong arm.

Meanwhile, in Uruk, Gilgamesh and Enkidu were arguing. They did this often, and had become good friends, but many who watched wondered at the bravery of Enkidu the wild man, who still wore his tunic of pelts, even in the beautiful palace of Gilgamesh. No other advisor dared face the king's wrath save Enkidu. That day, the king had recently returned in triumph from a campaign to the north, and while all praised his victories and marveled at the huge number of slaves and gold he had brought back with him, Enkidu alone raised his voice in protest.

"I don't see why you need to keep conquering more cities, Gilgamesh." He said gruffly. "You have already taken more land than many can see in a lifetime. What is the point?"

"The point," snapped the king, "is to bring order to a chaotic world. Life under my rule is so much better than that beyond my borders, and so I seek to help those out there by bringing them under my cloak of care."

"There will always be chaos." Replied Enkidu. "No one man could change that. You may have won battles along the banks of the Euphrates, but what of the Zagros mountains to the west? What of Humbaba, the mighty ogre? I don't see you trying to civilize him!"

"Enkidu!" Chided Tizqar, one of Gilgamesh's financial viziers "No-one dares go to the Zagros. That is the realm of monsters, not of men."

The king bridled at this. "Are you saying that I am afraid, Tizqar?" The man blanched and stepped away, shaking his head. "And you, Enkidu, you are right. I do not attempt to civilize Humbaba, but I will do better: I shall cleanse this ogre filth from the Zagros and his rich cedar forests shall be ours!"

Enkidu shook his head in despair. "I was not asking you to defeat this ogre, Gilgamesh, but to see that we all have limits. It is wiser to see those limits as they arrive, not to leap across them as over a stream, only to find that the farther bank is made of mud, not of stone."

His brows like thunder, Gilgamesh rose from his throne. "I may not be two thirds a god, but certainly I am descended from divinity!" He roared, and even Enkidu was silent. "I shall go alone to the Zagros, and I shall not return without the head of Humbaba!"

As the rising sun turned the white-washed walls of the houses of Uruk red, Gilgamesh spurred his horse forward, behind him trotted another horse, laden with supplies. He rode in light, leather armor, not the shining bronze of his battle gear, which was heavy and not for swift movement through trees. Alone he rode out of the great gates but stopped as a clatter of hooves made the paving stones behind him ring. Enkidu, also mounted, reined in beside him, still in his usual, simple clothing. "I'm going alone." Said Gilgamesh.

"Doesn't look like it to me." Replied Enkidu. "For one thing, you've got a horse between your legs."

The king couldn't help but laugh. "You don't have to come with me."

"I know," replied his friend, "but if you do slip on the other side of that stream you're about to leap over, I don't want you to get wet."

For many days they rode west and north, towards the Zagros mountains, which lay like a dark blue line on the horizon. Soon they could see the snow-capped peaks and the dark sides, thick with forests. "Humbaba's forest lies deep in that range." Said Enkidu. "Tizqar was right about one thing, men do not venture there: there is great power in those valleys. The gods alone can wander there without fear."

Gilgamesh nodded. "Once on the mountains, we must perform dream rituals to keep our minds sane. They may also show us our route and inspire a way of defeating Humbaba."

As they entered the shadowed vales of the Zagros, their thoughts became clouded. Both Gilgamesh and Enkidu had lived their lives out on the open plains of Mesopotamia, and therefore both found that they did not like being surrounded by mountains. "I feel shut in," shuddered Enkidu as he eyed the gigantic masses of stone that loomed around them. His companion nodded, "It's as though giants built walls to shut the world out." That first night as they pitched camp, Enkidu strung a series of protective amulets on the trees around them, while Gilgamesh stoked the fire and threw on a strange powder he had had prepared by Jushur, the high priest of Anu. "We must inhale the fumes from the fire," he explained, "and then go to sleep holding a weapon."

"That's part of the ritual?" Asked Enkidu.

"No, it's common sense." Smiled his friend. "The powder and the amulets are the ritual."

And so, having done their best to breathe in as much of the foul-smelling smoke as they could, the two wrapped themselves up in their blankets and went to sleep, hands firmly closed around their spears.

As he slept, Gilgamesh had terrible dreams. He dreamt that the mountains surrounding them began to shake, while the sky darkened and a deep, throaty roar echoed from the depths of the forest. From the darkness above a thunderbird swooped, its wings flashing with lightning, and the mountains themselves crumbled on top of him. He woke with a start, cold sweat drenching his clothes. The forest was quiet, the mountains still stood tall, black shapes framed against the stars, and only his friend's snores disturbed the peace of the night. The next morning, Enkidu reported no such terrible dreams, but did not seem overly worried about Gilgamesh's vision.

"If anything, my friend: you are the thunderbird!" He grinned, slapping the king on the shoulder.

Humbaba the ogre knew something was wrong. Birds came, as though fleeing the setting sun, and told him of unsettling rumors in the forest; of strange creatures that walked upright, but with the feeling of lynxes hunting. Humbaba had only seen one man before in his life, and he had eaten him. Licking his lips in eager memory, he headed west with strides twice the length of a man's. Soon he saw the two men making their way up the valley towards him. The points of their spears flashed like a river in sunlight, but they moved, as the birds had said, with the care and confidence of predators. Humbaba wore a great cloak of black bear fur and carried a large tree branch as a club. He did not fear these tiny humans. Striding down the valley, he roared, "You have entered the sacred forest. There is no turning back !"

Neither Gilgamesh nor Enkidu had ever seen a creature so ugly as this huge monster that bore down on them. They had barely time to shrug their packs off and ready their weapons before Humbaba was brandishing his great club with both hands. The first swing made Enkidu duck, while Gilgamesh lunged with his spear, managing to scrape his weapon up the ogre's forearm. Humbaba growled at the sudden pain, and backhanded the king, who did not dodge back soon enough and was sent sprawling a little way down the slope. Enkidu, armed today with a spear rather than his usual staff, jabbed at the monster's side, and then leaped back to avoid another vicious blow.

Gilgamesh was back on his feet, running back to help his friend. The two of them circled the ogre, Enkidu going left, the king to the right. But Humbaba had seen too many deer go down to wolves like this to be tricked. He made a feint, pretending to swing again at Gilgamesh, but then dodging back to strike at Enkidu. He roared his victory and shook the trees with his voice. But a pain in his leg cut his bellow short.

What had seemed to him to be an easy trick was child's play to an experienced warrior like Gilgamesh, or a wide-traveled man like Enkidu. They had seen Humbaba's slow mind forming his plan and a simple glance between the two of them had lain the trap for the mighty ogre. When he had lunged at Gilgamesh, the king had pretended to leap aside, but seeing the monster's head already turning back to his friend, Gilgamesh had merely stepped half a pace back, and then thrown his full weight behind his spear, plunging it straight through the monster's thigh. Wrenching the blade free, the two of them stepped back as the wounded ogre fell to the floor, clutching at his leg as dark blood slopped through his massive, clumsy fingers.

Normally Gilgamesh would have simply stepped forward and finished his prey off, but there was a childlike confusion in the ogre's eyes that brought a strange lump to the king's throat. "What are you waiting for, my king?" Grinned Enkidu, leaning on his spear. "You wanted to take back this creature's head, so now is your chance!"

"Mercy!" Begged Humbaba, and the two of them turned to him. "My strength is leaving me..." Mumbled the ogre as he tried in vain to stem the bleeding. "Please, I shall be your servant." He nodded at the vast trees standing all around them. "You want wood? I will cut it for you. I will bring it to you. Please, help me."

Still the king hesitated, and so Enkidu gripped him roughly by the shoulder. "You said you wanted to bring order to your lands. How can an ogre be part of that order?"

"And you told me to know my limits. This is not my land, and so my law does not apply here." frowned Gilgamesh, "This would be murder."

Enkidu rolled his eyes. "That is what you want to tell your subjects? That murder is only murder where your law holds sway? How can any citizen safely travel beyond your borders if they cannot go knowing that you will protect them?"

Gilgamesh turned back to Humbaba, whose eyes, though slightly unfocused, were still staring at him plaintively. In one fluid movement, Gilgamesh drew his sword and swept the ogre's head off his shoulders. Wiping his blade on the creature's bear-skin cloak, the king shook his head slightly, as though regretting his decision. "He would have rebelled eventually." He murmured, as though trying to convince himself of that fact. They wrapped the head up in the bearskin and bore it away with them, both of them glancing over their shoulders every now and then, as though sensing unfriendly eyes watching them through the trees.

Chapter 6: The Curse of Ishtar

Of the many dingir, the lesser immortals, who still walked the land, none was more feared or more loved than Ishtar. She took the form of a young, beautiful woman with chestnut brown hair, long as a horse's tail. She had a husband, but all knew that it was not in her nature to remain in one place for long. One day she could be found guiding a woman into a new relationship, the next her soft-spoken counsel would lead two cities to war. Ishtar was always hungry for new conquests, be they in love or battle. Instead of a horse, she rode a mighty lion, a two-horned helmet adorning her head. No mortal saw her approach without trembling either with fear or excitement. No mortal had ever denied her wishes or ignored her advice, until today. Today, Ishtar had been refused and her rage burned like a flame.

Gilgamesh, king of Uruk, and his friend Enkidu the Wildman had long since returned to Uruk from their adventure in the Forest of Cedar. Some of the immortals, particularly Enlil, god of earth, had been angry at the death of Humbaba, who had been the forest's guardian. But Ishtar, intrigued by this new hero of men, had sneaked into the king's bedchamber. There she had lain in wait, like a lioness in the undergrowth who knows that a great bull will soon pass by. She was counted among the wisest of the dingir, knowing the hearts and minds of men: she often knew what they would do before they did. But that evening, as she lay beautiful and moonlit, Gilgamesh had returned to his room and found her. He had recognized her at once, but unlike so many other mortals before, he had not bowed before the beguiling dingir. No: he had turned her away. "I will neither serve you nor dishonor your husband!" he had shouted.

Her eyes flashing with sudden fire, Ishtar had warned him, "You do not know what you do this night, Gilgamesh of Uruk. I could have given you power and pleasure the like of which you can scarcely dream."

But the king had only laughed. "You don't understand men at all if you think that is all we want in life."

Ishtar had nearly killed him on the spot, but her mind, swift as a hawk, had seen a better course of action. Thus it was, that now she entered the palace of Anu, the sky-god, and made a request: "Oh mighty Anu, lord of the cloud-drifting airs, your brother Enlil is right: Gilgamesh, king of Uruk, has grown too arrogant. He must be taught a lesson, not only for the murder of dear, innocent Humbaba, but also for his aim to conquer more and more lands. He thinks to raise himself to the level of the dingir! How can we allow such arrogance to continue?"

Wise as Anu was, he could not see the true reason behind Ishtar's words: revenge. "What would you have us do, Ishtar? I will not sanction another flood, even if this mortal's impudence is as you say, he alone should suffer."

Ishtar smiled broadly, "Oh, I can promise that he will suffer, great Anu. Give me your great bull, and I shall act as our agent."

Anu frowned. "But that bull will drink the rivers dry and cause a famine that will last for seven years!"

The cunning dingir raised her hands to placate him, "I have already made arrangements to protect the grain stores and the rivers, my lord." She lied, but such was her guile and so sweet was her smile, that Anu himself was deceived. Satisfied, the sky god bowed his head, and the next day, Ishtar led the prize bull of the gods down into the lands of Uruk. Golden were its hooves, silver was its hide, and its horns were of adamant, long and lethal.

Under Ishtar's command, the bull ran rampant through the pleasant fields and well-ordered orchards of Uruk. It tossed trees aside like matchsticks, crushed houses as though they were made of parchment, and drank whole wells and lakes dry in its thirst. Hidden in shadow, Ishtar watched and waited, for this was only the first stage in her plan to avenge herself upon Gilgamesh for his insult to her.

For the first time in his rule, Gilgamesh did not know what to do. On the borders of woods and forests and in the foothills of the mountains, wolf and bear attacks were common enough. But no-one had ever seen anything like this bull, which half-blinded those who saw it, so bright did its hide shine in the sun. "It can only be a message from the gods!" cried the priests, wringing their hands and pacing up and down. "We must pray and ask the dingir for guidance." Gilgamesh's generals, on the other hand, wanted to send the army after it, but the king shook his head.

"This beast has been sent by the gods. I will not send my men needlessly into harm's way." Standing, he cast his eyes around the council until they met Enkidu's steady gaze. "I shall face this bull. Now, all of you leave. I want every citizen within the walls of Uruk. There they shall be safe."

The lords and councilors filed out, leaving only Enkidu staring at his friend and king. "You know something about this bull." said Enkidu, his wild mane of hair and beard wagging as he shook his head, deep lines in his forehead dragging his wiry eyebrows tight together.

"I know nothing about it itself, but I can guess from whence, or rather, from whom it came." replied Gilgamesh sitting back in his throne and rubbing his temples, as though he had a headache. "The dingir Ishtar demanded I serve her. I refused, and now she has sent this bull to plague us. I brought this menace upon my people," Gilgamesh glanced at his friend, "and so I must bring it to an end."

Enkidu sighed deeply. "Well, I can't let you go alone, can I?"

Hidden within a shadow, Ishtar watched the two men as they made their plans together and laughed silently. Her plan was proceeding exactly as she had hoped.

Speeding along on a wide-based chariot, Gilgamesh and Enkidu followed the wake of destruction left by the bull. Their mournful eyes took in the splintered trees and the crumbling ruins of once happy homes. Enkidu had once thought that Gilgamesh was only interested in conquest and glory, but as he watched his friend urging the horses onward, his knuckles white on the reins, he knew that deep in the king's heart lay a strong desire to protect his subjects. They may once have been his enemies on the field of battle, but once they had bowed to him as king, Gilgamesh would spend his last drop of blood in their defense.

They found the bull drinking from the Euphrates and saw with horror that the river itself was running much lower than usual, such was the never-ending thirst of this divine creature. "Take the reins, my friend." instructed Gilgamesh. "And keep us moving." A thrill of excitement made Enkidu forget his fear as the king took careful air with his bow. The bull raised its shining head and its fierce eyes seemed to pierce the wildman's. Gilgamesh's bow twanged as the arrow flew straight into the beast's flank and a roar of rage blasted their eardrums. "Turn! Turn!" cried the king, and Enkidu wrenched his gaze from the bull's as it pawed the ground with one mighty, golden hoof. The horses screamed as they skidded around, Gilgamesh bracing himself against the side of the chariot firing arrow after arrow into the bull as it charged after them.

There were no horses faster than those born and raised free on the steppes and plains between the two great rivers, but this bull was overtaking them as though they were mere foals fresh from their mothers' wombs. As it drew up alongside them, the two companions had one fleeting glimpse of the furious red eye of the bull, before it barged straight into the pair of horses, its long horns tearing through them like knives through bread. Seizing their weapons, Enkidu and Gilgamesh leaped from the chariot an instant before it flipped over. They rolled over and over, feeling the thunder of the bull's hooves as it crashed around in a great arc. Leveling a throwing spear, Enkidu stood beside his friend even as Gilgamesh nocked another arrow to the string. As the bull crashed towards them, both let fly, and then dived aside as the beast swung its great head, horns as long as swords glinting and dripping with blood.

Gilgamesh got to his feet first, firing another arrow into the beast's rear leg. But the bull was faster than he expected, and already it was spinning around to charge again. As though time was slowing down, he watched it focus on him, saw the dust scatter behind its mighty hooves. Then Enkidu shouldered him aside, bracing a long spear in the ground and pointing it at the bull's chest. "Enkidu!" screamed Gilgamesh as the bull stormed past him, trampling his friend but catching the spear plumb in the middle of its steaming chest. There was a tremendous bellowing, but the beast was slowing, its breathing ragged. Without pausing to think, Gilgamesh grabbed his own spear and charged, plunging the blade deep into the creature's neck. With an almost sad sigh, the shining bull sank to its knees and then crashed over, the fierce light in its eyes fading like the setting sun.

The king's cry of triumph was stifled as he remembered his friend. He turned to see Enkidu, lying on his back, a gagged hole ripped in his side by the bull's horns. "No!" cried Gilgamesh, dashing to his friend and ripping his own cloak into pieces to try to staunch the wound. But a pale hand clasped his.

"It is over." Enkidu's voice, normally gruff and strong, shook as he regarded his friend. "The kingdom is safe once again."

Tears splashed down Gilgamesh's face as he watched the light fade from his companion's eyes. "You were my friend, I shall never forget you." He whispered, clutching Enkidu's slackening grip.

"But don't forget yourself." Breathed the Wildman, and then his fingers slipped from the king's hand, and Gilgamesh howled like a wounded dog.

Ishtar watched from a nearby hill. Anu would not be happy with the death of his prize bull, but at this moment she did not care. She could handle the sky god's anger. All that mattered was that Gilgamesh, who had spurned her, now felt more pain than he had ever thought possible. He had lost his best friend, and knew that it was, ultimately, his own fault. "That foolish king will carry this pain with him for the rest of his life." she said to herself. With a wide, cruel smile, Ishtar mounted her faithful lion and rode away.

Chapter 7: The Wanderings of Gilgamesh

There were many tales told among the people of Uruk. Some tales haunted the fires at festivals and told of terrible monsters and noble heroes. Some were kept for when a soft blanket had been tucked around a dear child who didn't want to go to bed just yet. But there was one which stirred the hearts of all, for it told of Utnapishtim "the Faraway" and his wife. Legend had it that these two, having survived the great flood of Enlil, had learned the secret of immortality. Somewhere at the end of the Road of the Sun, beyond a great, poisonous lake called "the Waters of Death", lived these two immortal humans still.

For weeks the people of Uruk and the lands around had been terrorized by a violent, seemingly divine bull with golden hooves and adamantine horns. But their king Gilgamesh and his trusted companion Enkidu had gone to hunt the nightmarish creature down. With bated breath the citizens waited, farmers and fishermen, soldiers and priests, men and women, all wondered what was happening, out beyond the high walls of the city. There had been no sign of the bull for days now, and while this was deemed a good omen, no-one could sit quiet and at peace for nothing had been heard or seen of their heroes either.

Then came a day when a guard on the walls, his eyes squinting against the bright sun, rang a joyful bell. Soldiers on swift steeds were sent forth, and crowds lined the main street. In through the gate came a trudging figure, bent backed, dragging a litter behind him. Upon the litter lay Enkidu, his normally frowning face peaceful in death. He lay upon the shining silver hide of the bull, which he and Gilgamesh had slain. Cheers of glory rent the still air, for the man who dragged Enkidu along on the litter was Gilgamesh, their king. Over his shoulder was slung the bull's head, its vicious horns glinting. The soldiers had offered to aid him with the litter, but one fierce glance had sent them to a respectful distance, and so Gilgamesh, king of Uruk, brought his friend home. And while all about him sang of his greatness and of his latest victory, no joy nor triumph filled his heart. His eyes were dry, for he had no more tears to weep, and his mouth was set in a grim look than none had seen before.

That evening they laid Enkidu to rest on a great bed of wood and straw, drenched in oil. The bull's hide was laid over him as a funeral shroud and Gilgamesh himself set the burning torch to the pyre. Smoke hid the stars above the palace, and when the sad songs had been sung, and all had gone home, still the king stood there, watching the black traces take Enkidu's spirit skywards. Knowing how close a friend the wild man had been to the king, Gilgamesh's viziers did not press their lord with affairs of state for a few days after the funeral. But even when he did finally return to the council chamber, it was clear that his mind was elsewhere, as though these were small matters that no longer caught his interest.

One evening, Gilgamesh sat alone in his throne room, staring moodily at the stool where Enkidu had so often sat. It was not just the death of his dear friend that troubled Gilgamesh so, although this was a pain that he did not believe would ever truly leave him. That morning he had noticed a single grey hair among the dark locks of his beard. There were creases in his olive skin which had not been there the last time he had glanced in a mirror. "I'm getting older." he sighed, and his voice was bitter. He stared hard at the short stool before him. "What would you say to that, Enkidu? Something smart and sarcastic no doubt, but true nonetheless." He gripped his knees, suddenly breathing hard. "I don't want to die, but it can happen so easily. It doesn't have to be a bull or a spear. I could fall from my horse or down some steps and that would be it."

Rising to his feet, he looked around the room he had once adored, having adorned it with gold and trophies from his many campaigns. Now all seemed hollow and pointless. Removing the golden circlet from his forehead, he tossed it aside contemptuously and left the room. Being a king wouldn't help him in this endeavor. Every child in Uruk knew the story of Utnapishtim the Faraway, the long-lived, but none had ever found him. "But I will." Gilgamesh promised himself.

Years had passed since that lonely moment in the council-chamber of Uruk, but still the fierce light burned in Gilgamesh's eyes. Long had he wandered in the plains and steppes and forests and valleys beyond Uruk. He had passed out of the lands he had conquered, until finally he had found the mighty bulk of Mount Mashu. The lands around were desolate and savage and now he was clad in skins of lion and bear. His hair and beard, once sleek and well-cared for, were now long and matted, just as Enkidu's had been. Casting his eyes up the mountain, he saw that it had two peaks that pierced the sky like the fangs of some terrible predator. Undaunted, Gilgamesh climbed the mountain which, if the stories were to be believed, no man had set foot on since the days of Atra-Hasis himself.

Finally reaching the snow-strewn summit, Gilgamesh found himself facing no dingir nor mountain goats. There was no gateway to heaven or even a mountain cabin. There was only a cave and at its mouth stood its two guardians, but they were nothing like any monster Gilgamesh had yet seen. Like giant scorpions they were, with black scales and terrible claws, their sting-laden tails arching high over their backs. But the eyes that regarded him were not fierce nor cruel. Indeed, they reminded him of Enkidu.

"A human!" muttered one.

"I can see that!" replied the other.

"We should ask him what he's doing here." said the first.

"I was just about to!" snapped the second.

Gilgamesh stepped forward. "I am Gilgamesh, and I come seeking he who is faraway: Utnapishtim."

"He's looking for Utnapishtim!" the first scorpion told the second.

"Do you think I'm deaf?" shouted the second scorpion.

"Well, you didn't tell him that the Road of the Sun lies though the cave, did you?" grumbled the first scorpion.

The hero's heart leaped. "That's the Road of the Sun? May I go through?" he asked, stepping nearer, almost forgetting that he was facing two giant monsters, such was his excitement.

"He wants..." The first scorpion began, but the second cut across him.

"I heard him! But it's too dangerous. He'll never get there. The lake will kill him if he steps foot in it!"

"Maybe he could work something out!" The first scorpion rolled its eyes.

As the two monsters continued to argue, apparently forgetting that the man was even there, Gilgamesh crept past them and into the cave, which led into a long tunnel.

Long as his journey to Mount Mashu had been, this stumbling journey through the endless dark of the tunnel seemed to be without end. He had brought only one torch and a few faggots of wood with him, and while they burned well and he jogged along as best he could, all too soon he was watching the last flame fade into glowing embers. Plunged into darkness, he had no choice but to keep going, one hand on the wall, the other out in front of him, feeling his way. "How this can be called the Road of the Sun?" He muttered more than once.

It was night when he finally came to the end of the tunnel, but the moonlight was dazzling to his eyes. Before him stretched a wide lake in the center of which he could just see a small island. Although no tale told him he was correct, Gilgamesh knew in his heart that if

Utnapishtim was anywhere, he was on that island. Remembering the scorpion's warning about the lake's water being deadly, he cut down several trees and built a raft. Carefully pushing it into the water, he hopped on board and rowed out into the Waters of Death, just as the sun inched into the sky.

As he neared the shore, Gilgamesh's heart began to hammer against his chest, for clear against the sand he could see the figure of a man, bent with years, his long beard tucked into his belt. Shaking with excitement, he rowed faster, and soon was standing on the island's crisp sand. "Are you Utnapishtim?" He panted, staring at the wizened old face.

"I am." creaked the sage. "And I can guess why you have come."

Suddenly, Gilgamesh felt awkward, like a child who has been discovered sneaking into his mother's pantry. "Can you tell me the secret to eternal life?"

Sighing sadly, Utnapishtim shook his aged head. "It was a gift granted only to me, not even, as the stories have been told, to my wife. I was afraid of death, and so asked Enki to let me live forever. But in doing so life lost its meaning. I have seen so many sunrises that their beauty no longer moves me. Every day has become like the one before. I have seen the world from end to end, and nothing surprises me anymore. You have come a long way, young man, but for nothing. I would not even wish this endless existence upon you, for in reality it is a curse worse than anything I could ever have imagined. Go home, and do not seek to fight your fate. Life is short, and joyous thereby."

The shoulders of the great hero had drooped when he had heard the old man's words, but then he straightened, as though a great weight had been lifted from his heart. He turned to watch the sun rise higher, and marveled at the bright flecks on water's surface. "It is a beautiful world." He told himself. "And I would be sad to tire of it."

He thanked Utnapishtim for his kind advice and, reboarding his raft, set off for home. He strode back through the long, dark tunnel, and passed the two scorpions who were, unbelievably, still arguing. Trudging down the mountain Gilgamesh stopped suddenly, as Enkidu appeared before him, whether a ghost or a strange trick of his mind he did not know.

"Did you really have to come all this way just to be told that?" the wildman asked gruffly. Gilgamesh smiled. "I guess it's the journey that matters, not the destination."

Enkidu scowled. "I'm the one who's supposed to have the last word, particularly if it's sarcastic!"

A strange feeling rumbled in Gilgamesh's chest, and he found himself laughing for perhaps the first time in years. "It's good to see you again, old friend, even if this is just a dream. But now, I need to go home. There is so much still to do in Uruk, and I've been away far too long."

Part III: Norse

THE ASH YGGDRASIL.

The Ash Yggdrasil

Chapter 1: Yggdrasil and the Nine Realms

T he Aesir say that they began it. They were the sons of King Borr, and for them mighty is too feeble a word. It is true that they had dragged the land from the depths of the sea. It is true that they had built the first mead halls, the first longhouses, and the first palisades to keep the wolves from the flocks. But when the lords of the Aesir went to council, they went to Yggdrasil. Yggdrasil is an ash tree, but greater than any fathomable by mortal mind. Indeed, Asgard, the realm that the Aesir called home, was but one of nine worlds that rested in the boughs of Yggdrasil like hanging fruit, for it was the tree of worlds. Three roots it had, strong and deep delving, which were fed by the two wells Uroarbrunn and Mimisbrunn, and the sacred spring Hvergelmir.

One need only look past the clouds at night to see that the universe, and thus Yggdrasil, is vast beyond imagining, but here are the nine realms of which the Aesir have told tales:

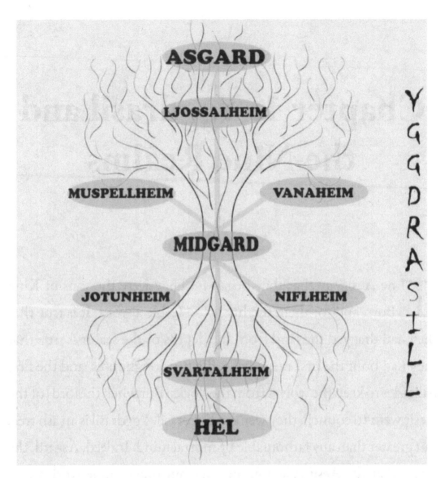

The first is Asgard, where Odin, the one-eyed Allfather, reigns over the Aesir in his meadhall Valhalla. Here come half those who die in glorious battle, while Freya welcomes the other half to her field of the host, the Folkvangr.

The second is Vanaheim, whence come many fair and wise folk as well as spirits of tree and spring. Some call these people Vanir.

The third is Alfheim. Here can be found the elves of light, fairest of all living beings. But they are remote, and care not for the lives of the other realms.

The fourth realm is called Midgard, for it lies near the heart of the great tree. Humans call this fair place home, and the Aesir visit it often, unsure if they prefer it to Asgard.

Jötunheim is the fifth realm, a land of ice and snow and glaciers that reach the sky. Giants dwell there, and other great and monstrous beings, though all are called the Jötunn.

The sixth is Muspelheim. It is as hot and sulphurous as Jötunheim is cold and icy. Surtr, the king of the fire giants, guards his people with a blazing sword, waiting for his time to come when all nine realms shall burn. He calls this time Ragnarök.

The seventh realm is Svartalfheim, where the dark elves reside. As ugly as the light elves are fair, they hate all living creatures.

The lowest of the nine realms is Niflheim. Forever shrouded in mist and fog, here rules Hel, who takes care of all those souls who did not die in glorious battle.

The ninth realm is Myrkheim. A dark world with halls of gold, here work the Dwarves, the finest craftsmen in all the realms.

Thus do ancient tales report the nine realms. But mighty and wise though the Aesir may have been, even they needed a method of traveling from branch to branch, navigating the endless reaches of Yggdrasil. And so it was that they built the Bifrost: a bridge of rainbows which would carry them wherever they wished to go.

Of the many tales of the deeds of the Aesir, the one that seemed most wondrous to the younger among them was the tale of how Odin lost his eye. Many was the time that his sons Thor, the great-hearted god of thunder, or Baldur his firstborn, or Vidarr the

Vengeful, would drink with him in the evening while the longfire spat and cracked. Then one of these three would say to their king, "Allfather, we crave to know how it was that you lost your eye. Was it when you defeated that father of catastrophes, Ymir? Or during some great campaign against the Jötunn or the dark elves? Did some dragon claw it from your head or was it taken in punishment for some past crime?"

And Odin smiled for he never grew tired of telling tales to his sons, hoping that they might learn from his wisdom and his follies in equal measure. So, he would call for the drinking horns to be filled once more and stare with his remaining good eye into the depths of the fire. Then, when the halls of Valhalla had grown still in anticipation, the king of Asgard would begin his tale.

"When we are young, my sons, we are always hungry. As babies we cry for our mother's milk; as checky boys we dare to look over that next hill; as foolish, would-be fighters, we snap at each other, testing for glory. When I was young, my sons, and yet already older than any of you can possibly imagine, I was hungry. Glory I already had, and honored was my name far beyond these halls. But still I was hungry. Gold flowed from my fingers and many were the ships in my broad harbour. But still I was hungry. My spear, Gungir, was well-sated with blood, and my belly was always full.

"My sons, I hungered for knowledge, and my thirst for wisdom could not be quenched. And so, I wandered wide and far, and I saw many things, and I spoke with many people. Across the Bifrost I strode, and while none dared stop me, nor would anyone refuse to answer my questions, still I wanted to know more. There are branches of Yggdrasil which I alone have seen. My eyes took in the sight of the unnamed eagle on whose brow sits the hawk Vedrfölnir. Only I have hunted the four stags who call the world tree their home, and they were fast even for me. I spoke with the squirrel, Rataoskr, who bears messages to that ungodly dragon Nidhöggr, who gnaws forever at the very roots of our mighty ash tree that knows no limits. Yea, even did I set eyes upon that foul beast itself.

It was at this point in the tale that one of Odin's sons, often Thor or Vidarr, would ask, "Why would a squirrel carry messages to a dragon?"

And always another of the brothers, usually Baldur the eldest, would cuff him who had asked around the ear and tell him to be silent. And Odin would smile and continue:

"But still I hungered for more, my sons. And so, I went to the base of Yggdrasil, to the place where the three Norns: Uror, Veroandi and Skuld, sisters from Jötunheim, ever bring water to keep the world tree refreshed. These sisters know what was and what will come. It was they who came to your mother when each of you came into the world and told us part of your fates. I asked these three, these Norns, how I could gain wisdom greater than all beings mortal and immortal. And they sent me to the highest point of Yggdrasil, telling me to hang upside down for nine days and nine nights, and then to go to the well of Mimir, the Mimisbrunn, where one of the three roots of Yggdrasil d elves deep.

"I did as they bid me, and I hung for nine days and for nine nights without pause. And then I came eagerly to the Mimisbrunn. But each time I tried to cup water in my drinking horn or with my cupped hands, my throat stayed dry. Then a voice, as though from the water and from the root, or even from within me – to this day I do not know – echoed in my mind. And it said to me, "With this water you shall see further than any before or after you. But to see such things will cost half your sight." And then I knew, my sons, what I must do. I must take out one of my own eyes in offering to the Mimisbrunn. It pained me greatly, for now in battle I am weakened and must trust my shield brothers and shield sisters all the more. Nevertheless, I took out my own eye, and sent it deep into the well of Mimir. Thus, I was allowed to drink from that water, and so it was that my mind was cleared and my sight was opened more fully than ever before."

When Odin, the Allfather, finished telling his tale, always one of his sons would ask, "Is this why you gave the gift of writing to the mortals, Allfather? And why you always tell us these stories?"

And Odin would nod. "A one-eyed man may be king in a city of blind men, my sons, but better yet to help them see, if only a little."

Chapter 2: The Gifting of Mjöllnir.

Of the many lords of the Aesir who lived in Asgard, none was craftier or more cunning than Loki, the shape-shifting god of mischief. A firm friend to his fellow gods, Loki was, however, always plotting something. His ingenious mind could not help but take him down curious paths, many of which ultimately helped the Aesir, but often enough caused arguments among the peoples of the nine realms.

One day, Loki had the idea to create a cloak of invisibility, but for this he would need the most perfect strands of hair to weave the subtle fabric. His eyes fell upon Sif, wife of Thor the thunder god, and her glorious, golden hair which glowed in the sunlight, and he could not resist the chance to see his plan through. He imagined, for a moment, what amazing opportunities would be open to him, if he could walk unseen even by Odin. So, that night, he took the form of a sharp-beaked raven, flew silently up to Sif's bedchamber, and cut the hair from her head as she lay dreaming.

On waking, however, Thor and Sif knew exactly who must have stolen the hair, and Thor, his beard crackling in his wrath, found Loki skulking in his workshop. Thrusting him against the wall with one massive hand, Thor boomed, "Find a way to return my wife's hair, or I shall shatter every bone in your body!" With a disgusted shove, he sent Loki sprawling on the floor and left.

"Even I can't restore Sif's hair." Muttered Loki, brushing himself down and beginning to pace up and down. Then he snapped his fingers. "But the Dwarves might! But how to persuade them to..." As the solution leaped into his mind, he almost jumped for joy. "That's it!" he cried, flinging his cloak around his shoulders and sprinting out the door. Calling upon the Bifrost, the great bridge of rainbows that the Aesir used to travel between the realms, he journeyed to the dark world Myrkheim. Here dwelt the Dwarves, the most skilled smiths of all the free peoples who dwelt in the shadow of Yggdrasil.

Hiding his mischievous smile, Loki went first to Idi and Egil, two brothers who claimed often to be the greatest of their craft, even in Myrkheim. On entering their forge, Loki bowed respectfully to the two smiths. "Sons of Ivaldi, I bring tidings: Brokk and Eitri, the sons of Sindri have promised to make three gifts for the lords of the Aesir to prove, once and for all, that they are the greatest smiths in the nine realms." As he expected, frowns ruptured across the two dwarves' fa ces.

"We shall prove them wrong then!" Grunted Egil turning to the forge and beginning to crank the bellows.

Catching his brother Idi by the arm, Loki said, "I tell you this in confidence, for it concerns the honor of Lady Sif: Some unknown thief has stolen her precious golden hair! Because your incredible skill has so often aided the Aesir, I do not mind giving you a hint: I can imagine that she and her husband Thor would vote for whoever could right this terrible wrong." Smiling at Idi's toothy grin, Loki swept from the workshop.

"Now for part two!" He whispered to himself. Coming to the home of the twins Brokk and Eitri, Loki explained the situation to the two dwarven smiths, but this time he told them that it was Idi and Egil who had laid down the challenge. Brokk and Eitri looked at each other and then back to Loki.

"Idi and Egil are many things," said Brokk.

"But arrogant is not one of them." continued Eitri. "You cannot fool us, god of mischief."

Loki waved his hands, trying to brush their suspicions aside, "My good dwarves, I assure you..."

"We shall fashion the gifts and prove our greatness." cut in Eitri.

"And when we win," said Brokk, his grin identical to his brother's. "We shall claim your head as our prize!"

Loki's mouth opened and closed a few times, but he could not back out of this now. Nodding dumbly, he left the twins to their work, while his swift-witted mind darted between the two looming walls of doom: either Thor would turn him into a bag of broken bones, or Brokk and Eitri would use his head as a doorstop. "I don't like either option that much," he decided, "so I must ensure that Brokk and Eitri lose."

Working together on their magic forge, which they claimed could rival dragonfire in its heat, Brokk and Eitri strived to create their greatest pieces yet. Brokk manned the bellows; it was vital that he not miss a beat, for even a small change could have huge impacts on their results. The heat was tremendous and sweat poured down his arms and back. Through the crashing of Eitri's hammer, a tiny humming could be heard. He ignored it, even as a small black fly zoomed through the smoke to land on his hand. It circled around one of his knuckles then bit down hard, sending a jolt of pain through the dwarf's hand. Gritting his teeth, Brokk did not stop pumping. Then the fly whirred up to his neck, and bit him again. Grunting with the pain, Brokk kept pumping up and down, up and down. With an angry buzz, the fly landed on his eyelid and bit him a third time. This time, Brokk yelped and swatted the fly away, the bellows falling flat to the ground. Growling he swiftly seized the bellows and began pumping again. But Loki the fly, his work done, flew triumphantly out of the workshop.

Their labors complete, Idi and Egil, Brokk and Eitri brought their respective gifts to Asgard, and presented them before the lords of the Aesir. Bowing low, Idi and Egil handed Odin, the Allfather, a mighty spear called Gungir, which could pierce anything. Odin admired the weapon greatly and thanked the dwarves heartily. Their second gift was for Freyja, the goddess of prophecy and love. Handing her a small piece of folded cloth, Egil bade her unfold it. With a rippling whoosh, the cloth spread out wide and became a ship large enough for fifty warriors. With a flick of her hand, the ship folded back into the small cloth, which could fit in her own pocket. "Truly you are wonders of your craft!" exclaimed Freyja.

Loki allowed himself a small grin as Idi bowed low before Sif, wife of Thor, and showed her their third gift: hair made of purest gold. Sif, her shorn head covered by a scarf, let a small whimper of hope leave her lips as the two dwarves gently placed the hair on her head. Immediately, it took root, and Sif threw back her scarf as her new hair shimmered in the firelight, brighter and more beautiful than her own original hair had ever been. "Thank you, oh thank you!" she cried, hugging the two dwarves who went red and eyed Thor slightly nervously. But the god of thunder smiled at his wife's happiness.

Now it was the turn of Brokk and Eitri, who first came to Odin and handed him a golden armring of such intricate workmanship that even the Allfather was momentarily stunned. "You have many sworn warriors, mighty king of Asgard." said Eitri. "And a good lord gives gold to his men."

"Every ninth day," explained Brokk. "This ring shall create eight identical armrings, and thus you can reward your warriors without reaching into your own treasury."

"Such skilful magic has not been seen in Asgard in centuries." murmured Odin, barely able to take his one eye from the ring. "Thank you, master smiths!"

Revealing their second gift, the twin smiths presented Frigg, queen of Asgard, with a huge golden boar that could pull her chariot across the sky faster than any horse or eagle. The queen was ecstatic over the gift, and the two smiths accepted her gratitude humbly. They then turned to the huge figure of Thor, and presented their third gift: a great hammer with a curiously short handle for a weapon of its size. "Behold Mjöllnir, lord of thunder." They said, reverently. Loki butted in, "But master smiths! How can even so great a warrior as Thor use such a weapon? The handle is too short. Was there some mistake in its forging?" His crooked grin faltered slightly as he saw Brokk and Eitri's confident faces.

"This hammer," said Eitri, "shall never shatter, even in your mighty hand, great Thor."

"This hammer," continued Brokk, "shall never miss its mark, whether you strike or throw it."

"This hammer," Eitri's voice rose triumphantly as his chest heaved with pride. "shall always return to your hand and your hand alone!"

Thor's eyes widened in amazement, and the other lords of the Aesir murmured amongst themselves. "This is indeed a glorious gift, as one would expect of only the greatest smiths!" cried Thor, hefting Mjöllnir and marveling at its workmanship.

Odin nodded his agreement. "Idi and Egil, you have crafted wondrous things, and I honor you for them, but on this day Brokk and Eitri stand victorious." All applauded, even Idi and Egil. With identical evil grins, Brokk and Eitri turned to Loki.

"We have won your contest, Loki!" Said Eitri. "And as promised, we now claim your head as our prize."

Loki backed away a few steps, his mind racing. "You may have demanded my head, master smiths, but you never laid claim to my neck. Therefore, you have no right to separate my head from my body!" He bit his lip and then glanced at Odin who was stroking his long, white beard.

Finally, the Allfather spoke, a grin spreading across his face. "Loki speaks true. But in place of his head, he shall work your bellows for a year and a day in payment of his debt."

Everyone present laughed at the ashen-faced Loki was dragged off by the triumphant twins.

Chapter 3: The Wedding in Jötunheim

Throughout the nine realms which rested like fruit in the boughs of Yggdrasil, there were few warriors as strong, brave, or ferocious as Thor Odinson, god of thunder, who lived in Asgard. Tall, broad-chested, with a thick beard and eyes as dark as storm clouds, it was said that no warrior could face him alone. While many preferred a spear or a sword or an axe, often with a shield, Thor wielded only his hammer, Mjöllnir, which had been forged in the fires of Myrkheim by the dwarves Brokk and Eitri. Aside from being beautifully wrought, Mjöllnir was special, even for a dwarven-made weapon, for its makers had enchanted it three times. First that it would never shatter, even in the hands of the mighty Thor; second that it would always hit its mark, whether thrown or struck; and third that it would always return to Thor's hand. Despite Odin's best efforts, war was ever a plague throughout the nine realms, and Thor had sworn especially to protect Midgard, where the humans dwelt with their lush fields and sweet rivers. Mjöllnir in hand and the armies of Asgard at his back, he strode without fear across the Bifrost, defeating dark elves and Jötunn and goblins and dragons.

At that time, the king of Jötunheim was a giant called Thrym. Before the crafting of Mjöllnir his forces had raided and plundered the nine realms. But now, Thor seemed unstoppable. And so, the cunning mind of Thrym thought of a plan, and the stout heart in his chest drove him to carry it out with daring speed. There came a night on Asgard without a moon. Even the stars were veiled behind the clouds as Thrym and three of his most trusted companions snuck into Asgard, past the sentries of the palace and into the very mead hall of Odin itself, Valhalla. Barely daring to breathe, Thrym crept into the bedchamber of the thunder god, and stole the mighty hammer which had slain so many of his people. The four fled, and when morning came, all of Asgard was woken by the roars of rage which threatened to crack the walls of Valhalla. Lightning crashed from hilltops and thunder boomed across the sky, rolling the storm clouds while rain and hail lashed the wide green fields of Folkvangr, where Freyja welcomed half the glorious souls who died in battle.

It took the calming counsel of Frigg, Thor's own mother, to soothe his temper long enough for him to sit in council with the lords of the Aesir. "Give me the armies, Allfather." Thor begged Odin; his knuckles clenched on the arms of his chair so hard that the wood splintered beneath his fingers. "I shall raze Jötunheim to the ground for this dishonor."

"We don't know that it was them, my son." Odin replied calmly. "I shall send my raven, Huginn to King Thrym at once to learn what truth may be found."

Thor ground his teeth. "Thyrm is a liar and a coward. He will hide Mjöllnir and deny his part in the theft."

But there Thor was quite wrong. Within days of leaving, the great black wings of Huginn could soon be heard again, and he bowed low before the lords of the Aesir before speaking.

"King Thyrm of the Jötunn sends this message:

Greetings Allfather, we do not deny the theft of Mjöllnir. It now lies buried deep in my palace, where even your finest wizards cannot find it. It pains me that it must come to this, but the warmongering of the Aesir has gone on for too long. I suggest this: for the return of the hammer, we offer something infinitely more valuable: peace. O-ffer me the hand of Freyja in marriage, join our houses in blood, and blood shall never again be spilled upon the fair leaves of Yggdrasil."

Huginn squawked with fright as Thor crashed to his feet and hurled his chair across the room in rage. "This means war!" His eyes blazed at his father. "Surely now you must agree?"

Odin ignored his son, and turned, instead to Frigg. "Will you accept these terms?"

The goddess of love and prophecy drew her feathered cloak tighter around her. "Are you insane, my lord? Firstly, I would never wed such a brute as Thrym. Secondly, do you not think this is his true aim: to gain access to my powers and magics? How more formidable will the armies of Jötunheim be if they know every move we make before we ourselves make it?"

"But with Mjöllnir in hand the threat is just as great!" shouted Thor. But Odin shook his head.

"I will not force her to wed, Thor. And she also happens to be right. Mjöllnir is a mighty weapon, but only your hand can wield it. The moment Thrym attempts to take it into battle you would simply summon it back. No, Freyja is more valuable than Mjöllnir. That is the end of it."

When the council was dismissed, Loki, god of mischief, took Thor aside. "My friend, there is another way." he said, smiling.

"You heard the Allfather," growled Thor, "we are forbidden to attack the Jötunn and Freyja will not consent to a trade."

"I'm not suggesting we trade Mjöllnir for Freyja." grinned Loki. "I'll explain on the way."

Thrym, king of Jötunheim, was excited. He had not expected to hear anything from the Aesir except war-trumpets and the sound of marching feet. But when a second black raven arrived, bearing news that Freyja was already on her way with her handmaiden for the wedding, he almost danced with joy. "Of course," he told his council excitedly, "I have no intention of returning the hammer. Once Freyja is wed to me, I shall have her re-enchant Mjöllnir so that it only responds to my hand, not Thor's. With her prophetic eye and the great hammer in my grasp, all the nine realms shall bow before us." But the raven was not Huginn, messenger of Odin, but the shape-shifting Loki, whose plan was now in motion.

Many days later, word reached the palace that Freyja and her handmaiden were finally approaching. Donning his finest clothes, Thrym ordered that a magnificent feast be prepared to welcome his new bride. When the two women entered the wide hall, Thrym saw that Freyja was tall and strongly built, her distinctive feathered cloak ruffling slightly as she walked, and a beautifully woven veil covering her face, as was fitting for a bride-to-be. "Welcome!" He said, taking her hand and seating her beside him. "I am glad that the Allfather saw sense." Freyja bowed her head, but did not say anything.

"Is there anything wrong, my dear?" Thrym asked. Freyja's handmaiden, a beautiful young Aesir leaned forward. "My lord king, the lady Freyja is tired from her long journey. We have traveled for many days and nights, for she was so anxious to meet you, noble lord, that she did not sleep a wink!"

A broad smile spread across the king's face. "Let us eat!" he cried, waving to his servants.

During the meal, Thrym respectfully did not question Freyja too much, but could not restrain himself as he saw her devour not only several salmon and a plate full of chicken, but also a whole leg of ox, washing the whole lot down with nearly a barrel of mead.

"My lady," explained the handmaiden again, "is starving. She was so excited about her impending wedding that she did not eat during our entire journey, even when I plied her with the sweetest fruits and the finest wine."

"Then let us not have her wait any longer!" smiled Thrym. Turning to his general, he ordered him to bring the hammer Mjöllnir.

"We shall be wed in its presence to consecrate our marriage." he explained, smiling. Although in reality, he wanted to make Freyja enchant the weapon as soon as possible.

Mjöllnir was brought into the hall and laid on the table before Thrym who turned to his bride. "Now, let us see your face, dear Freyja." He grinned. Raising the veil, he was astonished to find a huge, bristling beard and two eyes that burned like fire. "Thor!" He cried, backing away. Thor ripped away the veil and the feathered cloak, revealing his armor shining beneath it. Hefting the hammer from the table, he roared, "Time to die, thief in the night!" Thrym had scarcely enough time to see the handmaiden transforming back into the crafty form of Loki before Mjöllnir crashed into his chest, sending him flying into the wall. He slipped to the floor as dead as a stone, the look of shocked surprise still etched on his face.

Mighty though Loki and Thor were, even they could not face all the warriors of Jötunheim alone. Running through the terrified crowds, killing as they went, they leaped onto their horses and sped away, Thor firing thunderbolts over his shoulder as they went. They clattered across the Bifrost, which withdrew as they fled, cutting off the angry Jötunn who crowded at its base, flinging spears and axes uselessly after the retreating Aesir.

That night, the songs were high and the mead flowed freely throughout the halls of Valhalla. Even Odin laughed as he heard Thor and Loki tell their tale, the mighty hammer Mjöllnir resting on Thor's knee as he drank and clapped Loki on the shoulder. "You are a trickster, dear Loki, but I am glad you are our trickster!"

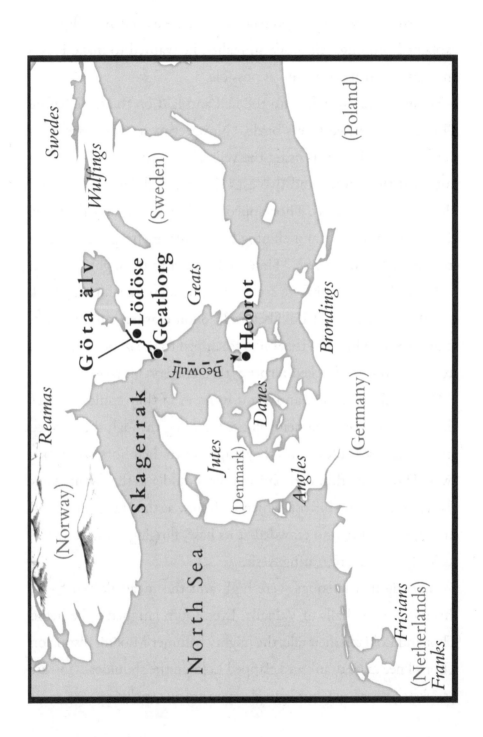

Chapter 4: Beowulf and the Slaying of Grendel.

On the realm of Midgard lay a land of rocky coasts and deep inlets called Danemark. Its people, the Danes, were ruled by an old, wise king called Hrothgar. He had been a mighty warrior in his youth and he still stood tall, but his beard was grey now and his hands no longer had the strength they once did. He had built a high hall, Heorot, and from there he dispensed justice, trained his men, and feasted. But across the land of the Danes there was cast a shadow: A beast which came in the night to halls where men had feasted. None saw it coming or going, for it left no-one alive. Hrothgar's heart was heavy, and although he sent his best warriors and his fleetest hunters across the land in search of the beast, they either returned empty handed or not at all. The Danes called the creature Grendel, and parents and children alike hid in their beds at night, shaking at every sigh of the wind or creak of a branch.

To the north of Danemark lay Scandza, a great land of mountains and rivers and fjords – steep-sided insets that provide safe havens for hundreds of longships. In this time there were many young warriors, sons of jarls who desired fame and glory for themselves. These men would gather together a crew, build a longship or saddle horses, and then see where the winds would take them, ever in search of battle. One such warrior was called Beowulf. The son of the king of the Geats, he had forsaken his father's fire, preferring to go viking instead. "If my name is to be remembered," he had told his father on the eve of his departure, "it will be because of what I have done, not because I was simply born your son."

Rumor drifted across the Skagerrak, the strait of water between Scandza and Danemark, bearing news of this Grendel, the shadow-walker whom no-one had seen, nor its wrath survived. On hearing the tale, Beowulf's eyes lit up as with a fire, and he called to his crew to load the longship with salted meat, twice-baked bread and ale, and to take up their oars. After days of sea spray and biting wind, Beowulf and his men sailed into the wide inlet, at the end of which, on a high hill, stood Heorot. On arriving at that great mead hall, Beowulf stood proud before the housecarls of Hrothgar, who demanded his name and his business. "I have come to rid you of the monster Grendel." Beowulf proclaimed, his chin high and his eyes ha rd.

After a short while, the housecarls let him enter, and even the hero sighed as the warmth of Hrothgar's hall washed over him. Approaching the king with a bow, he introduced himself again, and waited for the old man's reply. Hrothgar frowned from under his thick eyebrows at this young man from the north. "How is it," he asked slowly, "that you will succeed where the greatest warriors and the finest huntsmen in these lands have failed? How will you kill this monstrous creature?"

Beowulf smiled. "I shall not make their mistakes, lord king."

"Mistakes?" spat Hrothgar. "You watch your tongue, boy."

"It is a mistake to hunt this creature as you would a wolf." explained Beowulf, ignoring the king's chiding tone. "This Grendel does not hunt in the fields but in the halls of men."

The old king snorted. "Very well. If you think you can end this menace, then you have what blessing I can give."

Beowulf bowed his thanks. "Then, lord king, you and your people must leave Heorot. For tonight my men and I shall feast here."

"Leave?" Shouted Hrothgar, rising unsteadily from his chair.

"It is your choice, of course." replied Beowulf airily. "But all those who remain must be ready to face the beast's wrath. As I understand it, the Grendel strikes only halls where a great feast and merriment were made. We shall draw this monster out and lay a trap for it."

Many of Hrothgar's people shared frightened glances and a whispering hissed around the hall. The king bowed his head. "Very well. Those who wish to remain and face this creature may, otherwise we shall go east to Roskilde where my brother has his hall." Stepping down from the throne, he met Beowulf's gaze with sharp eyes. "If this be some trick to steal my treasure, boy, there will be no place where I will not find you."

Beowulf laughed. "Dead men have no need for gold, lord king. If I am still here tomorrow, I think that I will have earned some of your treasure."

As evening closed in, Beowulf's crew brought ale and meat from their ship, for their leader would not touch the food Hrothgar's people had left behind. Putting on his armor, Beowulf stared round at his warriors with a firm look. "Some men drink ale because they like the taste. Others drink before battle to steady their hearts and their shaking hands. Some drink to forget their fears, others to forget their crimes. Whatever comes through those doors has slaughtered whole halls of drunken fools. Take a little ale with your meat, but do not get drunk, for your lives may well depend on it."

And so, they began to eat and sing. First they sang the song of Thor's march on Svartalfheim, where the armies of Asgard had routed the dark elves. Then they sang of the Valkyrie, fair warrior maidens in service to Freyja. These women rode winged horses, coming at the end of battles to guide the glorious dead either to the halls of Valhalla or the fields of Folkvangr. They sang of swords and spears, of swift ships, of the biting wind, and of eagles and ravens high above. They sang of battles won and treasure seized, of glory and honor and oaths of friendship. As they sang, they stamped on the rush-strewn floor, beat their shields, clashed their spears, and laughed and roared their song to the night. And Grendal heard them.

Grendel. What a beast was he? Some called him a shadow-walker, others an ogre. Dark and hairy was his skin, his head an ugly block on a fat neck. Broad were his shoulders, long were his arms. His legs were as thick as tree trunks and his hands and feet were wide and awkward. Claws he had and fangs and evil eyes wide and staring. Sharp were those eyes and great was his strength. But keenest of all were his ears. He hated the loudness of men's voices, the coarseness and the joy in equal measure. His haggard heart hammered against his misshapen chest as the songs of Beowulf and his men echoed inside his skull. Growling with pain and rage, he set forth from his lair, forth towards Heorot with its high eves and well-tiled roof.

Beowulf was beginning to think that the beast would not come that night when something struck the doors of Heorot, making them rattle on their great iron hinges. As one, the men tossed aside their drinking horns and readied their weapons. Another blow sent the doors flying, and in stalked Grendel. Tall though the doorway of Heorot was, he had to stoop to enter. With bared teeth and flailing arms, he threw himself at the assembled warriors. Shouting, they attacked, but their weapons made hardly a dent in his thick hide. Hurling one warrior against the wall, he kicked out wildly, smashing the shield of another with his great, stinking foot.

Leaping forward, Beowulf tossed his sword aside and grasped the brute's thick arm. Grendel tried to throw him off, but Beowulf clung on twisting the creature's arm behind his back and bringing him to his knees. Still his men hacked and stabbed, but they may as well have used stalks of wheat for all the good their iron blades did. Grendel roared with pain and fury as Beowulf continued to twist his arm until, with a horrible crunch, he pulled the arm right out of its socket. Black blood poured from the wound and the monster screamed with agony. Striking out wildly with its remaining hand, it made a path through the warriors and barrelled from the hall, leaving a trail of blood in its wake.

"After it!" shouted Beowulf, and with hoarse cries, they chased after the beast. The moon was nearing its full, and by its light they could see the dark, bloody trail. Mortally wounded though their quarry was, they never managed to catch it, but followed the huge footprints until they came to a dark valley where nothing grew. In the center of the valley was a black, stinking lake, and there the trail ended, right at the water's edge.

"We can go no further." decided Beowulf. "No creature can survive such a wound." They returned to Heorot, where, in the morning Hrothgar returned with a dozen of his housecarls.

The old king was pale when he saw the doors of his hall lying splintered on the floor, and went paler still when Beowulf showed him the hideous arm he had ripped from Grendel's shoulder.

"In the greyness of yesterday I doubted you." said Hrothgar, slapping Beowulf on the shoulder. "But the brightness of victory brings new hope to our people. Gold shall be yours and glory in the lands of Danemark. Thank you, Beowulf." While all raised their drinking horns to toast the hero, deep in the dank darkness of the lake there was a cave. There lay the dead body of Grendel, but it was not alone. For every beast, even one so foul as Grendel has a mother. And that mother was already plotting her revenge.

Chapter 5: Grendel's Mother

B eowulf the Tall was a prince of the Geats, but he had moored his ship at Heorot, the high-walled meadhall of Hrothgar, king of the Danes. Days before, Beowulf had defeated the loathsome creature named Grendel, which had been terrorizing the land. Across the land, the news had run, bringing joy and a release from fear. Children felt free to laugh again, women sang in the evening, and men dared walk abroad at night once more.

But what none of them guessed, what none of them even thought possible, was that another creature could exist to torment them. For Grendel, like all creatures under the sky, had a mother. Like her son, she stood on two legs, but where he had been lumpy and misshapen, she was sleek as a snake, with a lashing tail and poisonous fangs. Together they had dwelt in a cave deep under a dark lake that stank of decay. Treasures they had; spoils ripped from the bodies of their victims. There it was that Grendel had escaped after his battle with Beowulf, and there, despite her attempts to heal him, he had died, gasping his last breath upon the filthy, bone-strewn floor. Then his mother howled, the coarse shrieking of her voice reverberating around the cave, shaking even the stones. Waiting for the night to break across the sky, she rose up through the foul waters of the lake and followed the bloody trail her son had left behind him, leading back to Heorot.

The feasting in celebration of the defeat of Grendel had echoed through Hrothgar's meadhall for many days afterward. The doors, which the beast had smashed in his attack, had been repaired, and the brute's arm, torn from his shoulder by Beowulf, hung now above the doorframe: a grisly reminder both of their darkest nightmare and their greatest hero. The warriors of Beowulf and of Hrothgar drank and sang together, arm in arm, and so it was that Grendel's mother found them, staggering around Heorot without a care in the world.

Unlike her son, however, Grendel's mother was cunning and cautious. She did not burst in, roaring with rage as her son had, but slunk up onto the very roof of Heorot, staring down through the smoke-hole at the revelry within. "There," she thought to herself, eying the great form of Beowulf who sat in honor at the king's right hand. "There is the foul being who killed my son. Let him come to me in my hall, and we shall see who sits smugly in victory then." With a terrible shriek, she tore open the roof of Heorot and leaped down among the drunken men and women. Slashing wildly, she killed many before they even realized what was happening. But as Beowulf leaped up onto the table, sword in hand, she seized two warriors and, with an evil grin, turned and bore her captives away.

"Thor, preserve us!" cried Hrothgar. "What foul fate is this? We thought we had been rescued from such evil, but now a second creature, more wily and fearsome than even the Grendel, has come upon us. What can we do?"

Beowulf sighed, staring down at the sword in his hand. "I must follow the creature and rescue our comrades. But this time, I will go into its very lair and chase out any others that lie hidden, thereby cleansing this land once and for all."

"That's madness!" shouted Unferth, one of Hrothgar's thanes. "It's a trap!"

Beowulf stared Unferth straight in the eyes. "You are right. It is undoubtedly a trap. But I go regardless."

If Beowulf hadn't already guessed that this creature had come from the same lake where he had followed the dying Grendel to, it wouldn't have mattered, for Grendel's mother left him a horrible trail to follow. Here and there, he found splatters of blood, and then a hand, ripped from its arm, or a leg torn and mangled on the ground. Clenching his teeth in rage and sorrow for the fallen warriors, he ran on until he came to that same dark lake which stank of death. Glancing up at the moon and stars for what might be his last time, he dived in.

Coming to the cave, he dragged himself out into its dark, stinking air and stared around. A fire had been lit at one end, and he saw with amazement the hoards of treasure piled along the walls. Bones littered the floor, and he half choked at the stench. But there was no time to pause. Before him stood the loathsome creature he had come to kill. Grendel's mother hissed, her terrible fangs bared in a horrible smile that sent shivers even down Beowulf's spine. Drawing his bright sword, he stepped forward.

Swift as a snake, the monster attacked, swiping left and right with her claws. Beowulf dodged aside, feeling them pass a hair's breadth from his throat. Slicing his blade down on her back, there was a clang of metal as his sword snapped in two. He had no time to stare dumbfounded at the iron shard protruding from the now useless handle, for Grendel's mother had rounded on him, her eyes alight with malice. Hurling the weapon at her, Beowulf managed to grab one of her arms as they tore through the air. Her breath was as foul as the water in the lake above, and his eyes watered as he struggled to heave her off him. Dodging aside again, Beowulf ran for the pile of treasures as his foe tumbled to the floor.

Amongst the many golden items that glittered dully in the light of the fire, one stood out from the rest. A shining sword, its hilt encrusted with rubies, lent against the dank, dripping cave wall. This sword could not have been made by men, so keen was its edge and so bright did it shine. Whether by a dwarf or fair elf it had been wrought, Beowulf did not know, but he grasped the handle and swung round to face his enemy even as she swung around, hissing and spitting. Seeing him with the wondrous weapon in hand, she hesitated for a heartbeat. Courage surged in the hero's heart, and he charged, yelling his battle cry and swinging the sword in a great arc. The creature's claws met the blade and there was a hideous yowl as those yellowing talons clattered down amongst the rocks and bones of the cave floor.

Beowulf swung again, and now the monster was retreating, swiping desperately at him with its remaining hand. With one last, furious lunge, he swept the creature's head clean from its shoulders. Green blood spurted from the wound, and Beowulf cried aloud in wonder and fear as the shining blade fizzed and hissed, melting away before his eyes until only the glittering hilt remained. Panting slightly, Beowulf looked around the cave. So much gold lay there, enough to build at least three more longships and pay the crews for a year. It turned back to the horrible corpse and shivered. Even in death, those eyes seemed to stare at him with hatred and hunger. Taking his cloak, he carefully wrapped the head up and dived back into the awful water. As his head broke the surface and he gulped down clean, fresh air again, he saw to his delight that the sun had risen, and a fair morning was gleaming with dewy radiance.

That evening, another feast was held in Beowulf's honor, and king Hrothgar laid his hands on the young hero's shoulders. "Lord Beowulf, your deeds shall be known across the lands and shall be remembered long after Heorot has crumbled into dust. But with this glory comes a great burden. For now, every man will think he knows you before he meets you. So the challenge you now face is not to fight monsters or ride the waves in a fleet ship but to maintain your legacy. Not just as a great warrior, but as a good man. Pride will sour even gold, and no warrior will follow a man who cannot see past his own greatness. Go well but go true to who you were when you first arrived here."

Beowulf bowed his thanks and, a few days later, having rescued the monsters' hoard from beneath the lake, he and his men sailed away. He had shared his gold well, keeping the majority for himself, but each man now had a shining golden armring on his right forearm, and they glittered as they rowed. At the prow of his longship there had been a wooden dragonhead, there to scare away evil spirits which prowled the waters. That dragonhead was now gone, but had been replaced by the skull of Grendel's mother, and the shrieking of the gulls might well have been mingled with those of the water demons that awaited unwitting sailors. Beowulf smiled as he felt the heave of the waves beneath his feet. "Sing men! Sing as we row."

And as one, the men caught up the song of the Windrunner, king of the sea eagles. A shiver ran down Beowulf's back, for he loved this song. He gripped the steering oar and added his voice to the chorus, glancing back at Heorot for the last time as it slipped into the mist behind them.

Chapter 6: The Dragon of Lödöse.

On the eastern border of the Skagerrak a stormy strait north of Danemark, lay the southern end of Scandza. Many rivers emptied into the Skagerrak, but few as bright or as wide as the Göta älv. Miles from the mouth, for one could row a long ship far upstream, there stood the city of Lödöse, where, on a high hilltop, stood the fortress of Geatborg, where Beowulf the Old ruled as his father had before him. Fifty years had passed since his name had rung across the seas, and people had gathered round the longfire in the evening to hear the skalds tell the story of Beowulf and the Terrors of Heorot. The hero himself was now grey of hair and beard, but he could still ride a horse and hold a spear steady.

Away in the wild hills above Lödöse, there was a deep cave, out of which smoke could always be seen to come. In this deep hole, there were many beautiful things. Cups and bowls of bronze and of silver and even of gold. Jewels glittered on sword hilts and belt buckles; well-polished suits of armor were stacked in untidy piles. Coins of every shape and size imaginable lay in heaps, and many precious gems were scooped into chests of oak bound with iron. But no king nor lord nor robber baron called this cave their home. There were no guards nor fortifications. Even the chests lay unlocked. No-one dared try to steal even a single coin from the hoard, for in this cave there lived a dragon.

Like a monstrous serpent with powerful legs and bat-like wings, the dragon knew no fear. Rust-red were his scales, thick as armor. His talons and teeth were as sharp as swords. On the wing, no horse could outrun him, no falcon fly faster, and the smoke that drifted from the cave's mouth came not from a fireplace piled high with logs and kindling, but from the dragon's own belly. He could blow flames from his mouth that would crumble a house into ashes in moments.

There came a day, however, when a young squire in the court of Geatborg lay alone in his room, tears of fright flowing down his cheeks. He had spent the night with the other squires gambling at cards, and now all his wages had gone, and he was also deep in debt to many of them. "If I do not pay them off, my position as squire will be forfeit and I must return home in disgrace." he moaned, head in his hands. "What can I do?" It was then that his eyes fell on the distant hills, just visible out the window. He remembered the tales of the dragon and its mounds of treasure, and a desperate idea came to his mind. Throwing a cloak about his shoulders, he saddled his horse and raced up into the hills.

He found the cave and blessed his luck to see that no smoke came from its depths. "The beast is either away or dead!" He whispered and crept inside. The tales were true! He gaped open-mouthed at the gold and jewels, more than a king's treasury. Then, coming to his senses, he filled his pockets with coins, more than enough to cover his debts, and then, for good measure, he took a beautiful golden cup. Sprinting back to his horse, he fled back to Geatborg, his heart light and fluttering with triumph.

That evening, the dragon returned to his lair after a long day of hunting. He had enjoyed the chase and was in a good mood, until he entered the cave and sniffed. There was a strange smell in the air, one that had not been there when he had left. Casting his eyes around, he saw that a pile of coins was much smaller than it had been before. And he slashed at the ground in fury, a golden cup was missing! Fire belched from his jaws, and he roared his fury to the night. "Thieves!" he boomed. "They shall pay!" Lifting into the air on his mighty wings, he flew, faster than the wind, to Lödöse. Folk screamed and warriors cried in fear as they saw his fury burning through the night. Arrows clattered uselessly against his scales while fire scorched the buildings and smoke curled into the sky. Seizing two men in his claws for his dinner, the dragon returned, snorting with triumph, to his cave.

Smoke still clogged the air the next morning as Beowulf walked sadly through the grey, ash-covered streets. "I do not know what caused this attack," he told his son, "but I'll be damned if I allow it to happen again. I shall lead a troop of our best men up into the hills and put an end to that dragon once and for all."

"Father," replied his eldest son, shaking his head. "Forgive me, but you are old. Let me go. It is what you trained me to do."

Beowulf laughed. "I trained you to fight men, not monsters. No-one in this land has more experience fighting such creatures than I do. Besides, you are the future ruler of Lösöne. You must be here to guide our people when I am gone. If I fall fighting, that will not be so sad a fate." He smiled and embraced his son, then ordered the thanes and housecarls to prepare.

Leading his men up into the hills above Lösöne, Beowulf turned to Wiglaf, his standard-bearer, looking down upon the green fields and the high walls of Geatborg far below. "I feel called, Wiglaf," he said quietly. "by what, I don't know." Wiglaf didn't know what to say to this and so stayed silent. Gripping tighter to the shaft of his spear, Beowulf wheeled his horse around and ordered his men to blow their horns. "Let this foul worm know we are here." he shouted. "Let it know its death approaches on the spears of Geatland's finest warriors!" The men cheered and blew their horns in a mighty shout that rang clear through the hills.

They did not have long to wait. From the north they heard a great beating, as though the sails of many longships were snapping in a gale, and then they saw it. The great, red-brown dragon swooped down upon them, its maw wide and smoking. Horses screamed, men yelled, and though every warrior there might as well have been born on a horse, so skilled were they at riding, only Beowulf and Wiglaf managed to control their steeds. The rest of the horses, eyes wide and mouths frothing with terror, careered down the slope, many throwing their riders as they went.

An awful sound of laughter rang in Beowulf's ears as the dragon landed not far from them. "Did you think to do battle with me, great king?" it growled. "Did you think that your little band of gallopers could possibly face me? Die now, Beowulf, king of nothing. Die and burn." And as it opened its great mouth to send forth flame, Beowulf, hero of Heorot, dug his heels into his horse's sides and charged, hurling his spear with all his might. The blade sank deep into the dragon's wing, and it roared its fury. Leaping forward, it swiped at him, knocking him from his horse and sending him flying. Drawing his sword, unable to rise, Beowulf slashed at the beast's face as it dived at him. But he might as well have slapped it with his hand.

Then a great shout came from his right as Wiglaf spurred his own steed forward. All his skill, strength, and speed were behind the spear's point as he charged headlong into the dragon, piercing it through the shoulder. Roaring with pain, the dragon opened its mouth wide, wide enough to swallow Beowulf whole. He could see down its throat, see the fire brewing inside. With the last of his strength, Beowulf lunged forward, stabbing his sword up into the roof of the creature's mouth. The blade shattered, leaving only a cracked sliver attached to the hilt. The dragon slumped down, its jaw gaping in a silent roar, the smoke from its nostrils suddenly extinguished. Then it keeled over, the furious light in its eyes fading into embers until they were as dull as grey coals.

"Lord king!" cried Wiglaf, leaping from his saddle and diving to his master's side. Beowulf smiled faintly. There was a great gash in his side where the dragon's claws had ripped through him, and he could no longer feel his legs.

"It is over, Wiglaf." he murmured. "I can hear the calls more clearly now. Look!" He pointed over Wiglaf's shoulder at something only he could see. "The Valkyrie come. They will bear me away to the meadhall of Odin, high Valhalla, and in the company of those mighty heroes, even Thor and Baldur, I shall not be ashamed to tread. Where is my sword?"

"In your hand my king." Wiglaf wept, clasping Beowulf's hand tight over the hilt of his broken sword, even as the king's fingers went limp in his grasp and those sea-grey eyes closed for the last time.

Finally, the other housecarls and thanes climbed back up to where the dread serpent and the noble king lay dead with Wiglaf still kneeling by his side. Removing their helmets, no man hid his tears. At last, Wiglaf stood. "Brothers of the sword. There will be time enough for grief. We must bear news of our great lord's death to his son, who now rules by right in Geatborg. Meanwhile, we shall build a great pyre to send Beowulf's soul to Valhalla. And all must take up the cry: Beware, great heroes of the Aesir, for here comes to you great-hearted Beowulf. A giver of gold, a just lord, a mighty king. He was the bane of the shadow-walkers and, at his last, the slayer of dragons!"

I hope you've enjoyed the book. Please kindly leave a review.

Glossary

Part I: Egypt
Gods

- Anhur (An-hurr): Egyptian god of war. Takes the form of a powerfully built man.

- Anubis (An-oo-bis): Egyptian god with the head of a jackal. God of funerals and transitions.

- Apophis (Ah-poh-fiss): Immortal enemy of Ra. A giant serpent that lives in the Duat and causes earthquakes when he moves.

- Geb (Geb): Egyptian "god"/personification of land, earth.

- Horus (Hor-russ): Falcon-headed son of Isis and Osiris. All human pharaohs claimed him as their ancestor.

- Isis (Eye-siss): Egyptian goddess of magic and cunning. Wife of Osiris. Takes the form of a beautiful woman with long feathers coming from her arms like a cloak.

- Nun (Nu-un): Egyptian "god"/personification of water, seas, the encircling ocean of the world.

- Nut (Nut): Egyptian "god"/personification of the sky.

- Osiris (Oh-sigh-riss): Egyptian god of agriculture and fertility. First king of Egypt after Ra, then king/god of the underworld/the Duat.

- Ra (Rah): The chief Egyptian god. God of the Sun. Falcon-headed.

- Sekhmet (Sek-met): Egyptian lioness-headed goddess of the sun, disease, and healing. Daughter of Ra and the "Eye of Ra". Fiery breath causes plagues.

- Set (Set): Egyptian hyena-headed god of storms and deserts. Often helps Ra battle Apophis in the Duat.

- Shu (Shoe): Egyptian "god"/personification of the air.

- Thoth (Th-oh-th): Egyptian god of the moon, wisdom, and magic. Ibis-headed.

Humans
- Anees (An-ees): An Egyptian man, husband of Neith.

- Neith (Nee-th): An Egyptian woman, mother of Mika, wife of Anees, daughter of Alin.

- Pharoah (Fair-row): The king or queen who ruled ancient Egypt.

Places

- Abydos (Ab-ee-doss): The site of Osiris' temple and palace on the Nile.

- Black Land: The rich, fertile area of Egypt around the Nile, where the river floods each year. Originally ruled by Osiris, later by Horus.

- Duat (Dew-at): The Egyptian Underworld; home of Apophis; kingdom of Osiris (eventually).

- Field of Reeds: The final goal of dead souls in the Duat: an endless, idyllic field where they could work in happiness without pain or stress, surrounded by friends and family.

- Red Land: The dry, sandy deserts beyond the Black Land of Egypt. Ruled By Set.

- Sea of Blood: The Red Sea.

- Sea of Calm: The Gulf of Suez, part of the Red Sea.

- Shesepibre (Shess-ep-i-bray): Site of Ra's palace at the head of the Nile Delta.

Animals & Monsters

- Amet (Ah-met): An Egyptian creature with the head of a crocodile and the body of a hippo. It dwelt in the Duat, eating the hearts of those deemed unworthy to enter the Field of Reeds.

- Scarab (sca-rab): A fat beetle.

- Sphinx (S-finks): An Egyptian monster with the body of a lion and the head of a human.

Items

- Book of the Dead: A scroll, written by priests of Anubis, which was supposed to guide the dead person's soul through the Duat.

- Kalasiris (kal-ah-sir-riss): Ancient Egyptian dress.

- Khopesh (kop-esh): Ancient Egyptian sword with a broad, sickle-like blade.

- Mandjet (Man-d-jet): The solar barge which Ra sails through the sky during the day.

- Mesektet (Mes-eh-k-tet): The solar barge which Ra sails through the Duat during the night.

- Pschent (P-shent): The red and white "double" crown of Egypt, bearing two animals' emblems - the cobra and the vulture.

- Was (was): A magical wand or rod, used by ancient Egyptian sorcerors and priests.

Part II: Mesopotamia
Gods

- Anu (An-uu): The Mesopotamian god of the sky.

- Dingir (ding-ear): A minor Mesopotamian immortal being.

- Enki (En-key): The Mesopotamian god of fresh water.

- Enlil (En-lill): The Mesopotamian god of the earth.

- Geshtu (Gesh-too): A dingir who rebelled against the three main Mesopotamian gods.

- Gishzida (Gish-zee-da): A dingir charged with guarding the gate of heaven.

- Ishtar (Ish-tarr): A female dingir with special power over love and war.

- Isimud (Is-ee-mud): A cheeky dingir with the power of the south wind.

- Ninhursag (Nin-her-sag): A dingir who was tasked with creating humans.

- Tammuz (Tam-muzz): A dingir charged with guarding the gate of heaven.

Humans

- Adapa (Ad-ah-pah): A priest of Enki living in Eridu.

- Aga (Ah-gah): Former king of Uruk.

- Atra-Hasis (At-ra-ha-siss): A wise chief of a tribe.

- Bazim (Baz-im): A human merchant.

- Enkidu (En-key-doo): "The wildman", friend of Gilgamesh.

- Gilgamesh (Gill-gah-mesh): King of Uruk.

- Jushur (Jush-urr): Gilgamesh's high priest.

- Leila (Lay-la): A human queen, mother of Zal, wife of Saam.

- Mehrab (Meh-rab): King of Kabol, father of Rudaba.

- Mesh-he (Mesh-he): An official of Gilgamesh in charge of

his building projects.

- Parum (Pah-rum): A mason working on Gilgamesh's latest building project.

- Rudaba (Ru-da-ba): Princess of Kabol, wife of Zal, daughter of Mehrab.

- Saam (S-aa-m): A human king, father of Zal, husband of Leila.

- Tizqar (Tiz-car): A financial advisor to Gilgamesh.

- Torin (Tor-rin): A miller from Eridu.

- Utnapishtim (Ut-nap-ish-tim): A man granted immortality by the gods.

- Zal (Zal): Son of Saam and Leila, an albino.

- Sumerian (Su-mare-ree-an): People who lived in the land of Sumer, southern Mesopotamia.

Places

- Eridu (Eh-ri-doo): A town on the banks of the Euphrates River.

- Euphrates (You-fray-tees): One of the two great rivers of

Mesopotamia.

- Forest of Cedar: A forest in the Zagros mountains.

- Hara Berezaiti (Ha-ra-Bear-re-zai-tee): "The High Watch-post" - a magical mountain near where, supposedly, the Tigris river flows.

- Kabol (Ka-bol): Modern day Kabul.

- Mesopotamia (Mes-oh-pot-ah-me-ah): Roughly the area encompassed by drainage basins of the Tigris and Euphrates rivers. Part of modern-day Turkey, Syria, Iran, Iraq, and Kuwait.

- Mount Mashu (Mount Mash-hu): A sacred mountain in Mesopotamia.

- Road of the Sun: A tunnel under Mount Mashu.

- Tigris (Tie-griss): One of the two great rivers of Mesopotamia.

- Uruk (Ur-ruk): A city on the river Euphrates, home of Gilgamesh.

- Waters of Death: A lake of poisonous water.

- Zagros (Zag-ros): A range of mountains in Mesopotamia.

Animals & Monsters

- Humbaba (Hum-ba-ba): An ogre living in the Zagros mountains, supposedly employed by the gods to guard a forest of cedar trees

- Simurgh (Sim-ur-g): A huge bird with copper wings and the head of a dog, which could talk.

- Thunderbird: A mythical creature which could cause storms.

Items & Misc.

- Vizier (viz-ear): A royal advisor in Mesopotamia

- Ziggurat (Zig-gur-rat): A pyramid-like building, often with a flat roof.

Part III: Norse
Gods

- Aesir (Aye-seer): The most powerful of the Asgardians, worshiped as gods by most of the nine realms.

- Allfather: A title of Odin.

- Baldur (Ball-durr): Firstborn son of Odin.

- Borr (Bore): The primordial king of Asgard.

- Freyja (Fray-ja): A female Aesir, goddess of prophecy and magic. Wears a cloak of falcon feathers.

- Loki (Low-key): Shape-shifting Norse god of mischief.

- Mimir (Mim-ear): A supremely wise being who created Mimisbrunn at the base of Yggdrasil.

- Odin (Oh-din): One-eyed King of Asgard; The Allfather.

- Sif (Siff): Aesir, wife of Thor.

- Skuld (Sk-uld): One of the three Norns.

- The Norns: Three sisters who can see the future.

- Thor (Th-or): Asgardian god of thunder, husband of Sif, son of Odin, wielder of Mjöllnir.

- Uror (Ur-or): One of the three Norns.

- Valkyrie (Val-k-igh-ree): A female spirit tasked with guiding the souls of those who have died in battle to Valhalla or Folkvangr.

- Veroandi (Ver-oh-and-ee): One of the three Norns.

- Vidarr (Vid-are): "The Vengeful" son of Odin.

Humans & Other Mortal Beings

- Beowulf (Bay-oh-wolf): "The Tall". A prince of the Geats. Defeated three monsters.

- Brokk (Brock): A dwarven smith, twin of Eitri.

- Dane (Dane): An inhabitant of Danemark, modern-day Denmark.

- Egil (Ee-gill): A dwarven smith.

- Eitri (Ee-tree): A dwarven smith, twin of Brokk.

- Geat (Geet): An inhabitant of Scandza, modern-day Sweden.

- Hrothgar (H-roth-gar): King of Danemark.

- Huginn (Hue-gin): One of Odin's raven messengers.

- Idi (Id-ee): A dwarven smith.

- Ivaldi (I-val-dee): A dwarf, father of Idi and Egil.

- Jötun/Jötunn (Yoh-tun): The inhabitants of Jötunheim. "Jötunn" is plural.

- Sindri (Sin-dree): A dwarf, father of Eitri and Brokk.

- Surtr (Sur-terr): King of the fire giants.

- Thrym (Th-rim): The king of Jötunheim.

- Unferth (Un-ferth): One of Hrothgar's thanes.

- Wiglaf (wig-laugh): Beowulf's servant.

Places

- Alfheim (Alf-high-m): One of the nine realms, home of the light elves.

- Asgard (As-gard): One of the nine realms, home of the Aesir, Thor, Odin, etc.

- Danemark (Dane-mark): Modern-day Denmark.

- Folkvangr (folk-van-ger): Freyja's vast plains of battle in Asgard where half the mortal souls who have died in battle go to fight without pain, awaiting Ragnarök.

- Geatborg (Geat-borg): The castle of Beowulf.

- Göta älv (Goh-ta-alv): A river in Sweden.

- Heorot (Heh-oh-rot): The meadhall of Hrothgar.

- Jötunheim (Yoh-tun-high-m): One of the nine realms, covered in ice and snow, home of the Jötunn.

- Lödöse (Low-dose): Capital city of the Geats, home of Beowulf.

- Midgard (Mid-guard): One of the nine realms, home of humans.

- Muspelheim (Muss-pell-high-m): One of the nine realms, a land of fire and volcanoes, home of Surtr and the fire giants.

- Myrkheim (Murk-high-m): One of the nine realms, home of the dwarves.

- Niflheim (Nif-el-high-m): One of the nine realms, a land of mist and fog. Ruled by Hel. Home of all souls who did not die in glorious battle.

- Scandinavia (Scan-din-ay-vee-ah): An area of land encompassing modern-day Sweden, Norway, Denmark, and Finland.

- Scandza (Sc-and-za): Modern-day Sweden.

- Skagerrak (Skag-er-rak): A strait of water between Denmark and Sweden.

- Svartalfheim (S-vart-alf-high-m): One of the nine realms, home of the dark elves.

- Valhalla (Val-hal-ah): Odin's meadhall in Asgard where half the mortal souls who have died in battle go to feast and await Ragnarök.

- Vanaheim (Van-a-high-m): One of the nine realms, home of the beautiful Vanir.

- Yggdrasil (Ig-dra-sill): "The Tree of Worlds", all worlds sit in its branches.

Animals & Monsters

- Dragon (drag-on): A flying, fire-breathing, lizard-like monster.

- Grendel (Gren-dal): A monstrous ogre which hates the sound of humans singing.

- Grendel's mother: Mother of the monster Grendal. Serpent-like with clawed arms and legs and poisonous blood.

- Nidhöggr (Nid-hoe-gear): The dragon which gnaws at the roots of Yggdrasil.

- Rataoskr (Rat-ah-os-kear): A squirrel which carries messages through Yggdrasil to Nidhöggir, the dragon.

- Vedrfölnir (Ved-er-fohl-near): The hawk sits on the head of the unnamed eagle which sits atop Yggdrasil.

- Windrunner: King of eagles.

Items & Misc.

- Bifrost (Bye-frost): The bridge of rainbows used by the Aesir to travel between the nine realms.

- Gungir (Gun-gear): Odin's spear.

- Housecarl (house-carl): A Scandinavian warrior in service to a lord or king

- Hvergelmir (H-ver-gel-mir): A sacred well which feeds Yggdrasil; where Odin sacrificed hver-gel eye in return for wisdom.

- Mimisbrunn (Mim-is-brun): A sacred spring which feeds Yggdrasil; where Odin sacrificed his eye in return for wisdom.

- Mjöllnir (M-yoll-near): Thor's hammer, which could not break, could not miss its target, and would always return to his hand.

- Ragnarök (Rag-nah-roh-k): "The twilight of the gods". The day when Asgard and the nine realms shall be destroyed.

- Thane (thane): A noble Scandinavian warrior in service to a lord or king.

- Uroarbrunn (Ur-oh-ar-brun): A sacred spring which feeds Yggdrasil.

10-MINUTE STORY SERIES

For 9-12years old

And more are coming soon ....

Scan the QR Code. Never miss a free newly released series.

Made in United States
Troutdale, OR
12/13/2024